THE BIBLE PROMISE BOOK

FOR ➡ TEENS

TIMELESS ANSWERS FOR TOUGH QUESTIONS

© 2018 by Steve Russo.

Print ISBN 978-1-68322-450-1

eBook Editions:
Adobe Digital Edition (.epub) 978-1-68322-799-1
Kindle and MobiPocket Edition (.prc) 978-1-68322-800-4

Bible permissions are listed on pages 281–283.

Published by Barbour Books, an imprint of Barbour Publishing, Inc., 1810 Barbour Drive, Ohio 44683, www.barbourbooks.com

Our mission is to inspire the world with the life-changing message of the Bible.

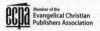
Member of the
Evangelical Christian
Publishers Association

Printed in the United States of America.

Steve Russo

THE BIBLE PROMISE BOOK®

FOR →TEENS

*TIMELESS ANSWERS
FOR TOUGH QUESTIONS*

BARBOUR BOOKS
An Imprint of Barbour Publishing, Inc.

CONTENTS

INTRODUCTION

A promise is a personal commitment you make and others expect you to keep. What promises are you making? Are you keeping them? . . .

There are three kinds of promises:
1. The promise you make but have no intention of ever keeping.
2. The promise that has conditions attached. (If things don't quite work out as expected, it's toast.)
3. The promise you're totally committed to keeping.

Unfortunately, there are lots of people who make promises; but few actually keep them. It's disappointing when you're counting on a promise someone made to you, only they don't deliver.

Relationships are based on trust, so it's tough when you have family or friends who don't keep their promises. However, there is someone who has never, ever failed to keep a promise—that someone is God. The Bible is full of His promises to carry us through when we need help. Promises you can always depend on. Commitments God has made to me and to you that He fully intends to keep.

The promises found in the Bible will change your life. The Bible has answers to the tough questions we have. Encouragement for when we're down. Hope for when we're feeling hopeless. Strength for when we feel weak. God's promises to guide us on the right path for our lives.

The wisest thing we can do is to read the Bible so we can know, understand, and apply the promises of God to our lives. God speaks to us through His Word, which is unlike any other book ever written throughout human history. If you're reading the Bible, you have no reason to doubt God. He won't always give us what we want, but He always does what's best for us.

This book you're holding is designed to be a resource to help you access timeless answers from the Bible to questions you have about life. Eventually you'll be able to share these answers with your friends, family members, and anyone else you hang out with who's also trying to make sense out of life.

It's going to take some time, careful thought, and a patient desire to hear God speak to you through His Word. But I'll tell you from personal experience—it's worth it.

God should be our first resource, not our last resort. Take time to thoroughly examine the portions of God's Word found on these pages. Make the Bible a priority in your life. Believe and act on the promises you discover. I guarantee you will never be the same as you discover God's real answers for your life.

There are lots of ways to use this book. For example, you can use it like a reference book to answer questions you have. The "APP" readings discuss life application for each topic. You can also read through the pages during your daily alone time with God. It can be used as a discussion guide for small groups at church or for a Christian club at school. Or, if a friend is searching spiritually, this is also a great resource to share with them.

I'm excited to have you join me on this journey to discover the awesome promises of God.

—Steve Russo

ABUSE

APP: *Sometimes I wonder if the way we think about abuse is too limited. Abuse comes in so many different forms. The default is most often sexual or physical. We hear about—and sometimes see—a lot of this kind of abuse, because it's the most obvious. It's often part of stuff (movies, television, etc.) that entertains us. Abuse can also be verbal and emotional. But people even abuse power, money, and fame. Have you ever felt as if someone you trusted abused your friendship? Any form of abuse can be damaging. Treating someone badly, being cruel, or wrongly using something or someone is never good.*

Using the following verses as a filter, take an honest look at yourself. If you've been abusive, ask God to help you change. Stop hurting yourself and others in your life. Let God guide you through the wisdom of His Word. And if you know others who have been abusive, pray that God would help you not to judge them but to influence them for good.

He frees them from tyranny and torture—when they bleed, he bleeds; when they die, he dies.

PSALM 72:14 MSG

"On that day I will punish every one who leaps over the threshold, and those who fill their master's house with violence and fraud."

ZEPHANIAH 1:9 RSV

For those who are evil will be destroyed, but those who hope in the LORD will inherit the land.

PSALM 37:9 NIV

If any think they are religious, and do not bridle their tongues but deceive their hearts, their religion is worthless.

JAMES 1:26 NRSV

The LORD also will be a refuge *and* a stronghold for the oppressed, a refuge in times of trouble.

PSALM 9:9 AMP

Thus says the LORD, "Do justice and righteousness, and deliver the one who has been robbed from the power of *his* oppressor. Also do not mistreat *or* do violence to the stranger, the orphan, or the widow; and do not shed innocent blood in this place."

JEREMIAH 22:3 NASB

Not requiting evil with evil nor abuse with abuse, but, on the contrary, giving a blessing in return, because a blessing is what you have been called by God to inherit.

1 PETER 3:9 WNT

The LORD tests those who do right, but he hates the wicked and those who love to hurt others.

PSALM 11:5 NCV

When [Jesus] was abused, he did not return abuse; when he suffered, he did not threaten; but he entrusted himself to the one who judges justly.

1 PETER 2:23 NRSV

For [the LORD] has not despised or abhorred the affliction of the afflicted; neither has He hidden His face from him, but when he cried to Him, He heard.

PSALM 22:24 AMPC

You will weep no more. How gracious he will be when you cry for help! As soon as he hears, he will answer you.
ISAIAH 30:19 NIV

"Peace I leave with you, My peace I give to you; not as the world gives do I give to you. Let not your heart be troubled, neither let it be afraid."

JOHN 14:27 NKJV

ADULTERY

APP: *Any way you look at it, adultery's ugly. And just in case you're wondering—I'm not talking about the studio albums that bands like Do-Re-Mi and Dog Fashion Discos have released titled "Adultery." The kind I'm talking about is epidemic—it's everywhere. Politicians are doing it. Superstar athletes, celebs, and even pastors are hooking up with someone other than their spouse. Even regular people living ordinary lives are caught up in this sinkhole of passion. It's hard to believe, but adultery is actually illegal in some places on the planet. Unfortunately, way too many families have been broken because a spouse willfully got involved in extramarital sex with someone. Lots of people say it's because they want to be happy. But this kind of happiness doesn't last.*

Because God is the One who designed the relationship between a husband and a wife, He has got some pretty strong stuff to say about sex that interferes with marriage relations. If we take His advice seriously, it will help keep us from experiencing the gut-wrenching pain of a future broken marriage. God's words can also lend a hand in mending your broken heart if your family has been shattered by disloyalty. It's all about deciding whether you want God's best.

But a man who commits adultery has no sense; whoever does so destroys himself.

PROVERBS 6:32 NIV

You have heard that it was said, You shall not commit adultery. But I say to you that everyone who so much as looks at a woman with evil desire for her has already committed adultery with her in his heart.

MATTHEW 5:27–28 AMPC

Let marriage be held in honor among all, and let the marriage bed be undefiled, for God will judge the sexually immoral and adulterous.

HEBREWS 13:4 ESV

And so the Lord knows how to rescue godly people from their trials and how to keep the wicked under punishment for the Day of Judgment, especially those who follow their filthy bodily lusts and despise God's authority.

2 PETER 2:9–10 GNT

**Those who love wisdom make
their parents happy, but friends
of prostitutes waste their money.**
PROVERBS 29:3 NCV

For God has not called us for impurity, but in holiness.

1 THESSALONIANS 4:7 ESV

ALCOHOL

APP: *Have you noticed how funny the beer commercials are on TV? I think some of the most creative minds around get hired to produce these sixty-second spots. And isn't it amazing how most of the time the commercials have very little to do with beer, yet we remember them anyway—which is exactly what the manufacturer wants us to do!*

But what the commercials fail to show are the guys building stomach muscles on the front lawn after a night of binge drinking or the girl hugging a porcelain throne 'cause she got drunk. You never see a picture of the wrecked car full of teens who died because of drinking and driving.

Drinking is made to look cool, and it's a way to escape the pain for a lot of people—but it can be very destructive. There's a better way to experience "cool" and deal with the pain of life. If this is a struggle for you or a friend, consider God's truth and advice. The guidance God gives us in the Bible isn't always easy to do, but it's always the best path to follow. Think through these verses and ask the Holy Spirit to help you apply the truths they contain.

Surely you know that the people who do wrong will not inherit God's kingdom. Do not be fooled. Those who sin sexually, worship idols, take part in adultery, those who are male prostitutes, or men who have sexual relations with other men, those who steal, are greedy, get drunk, lie about others, or rob—these people will not inherit God's kingdom.

1 CORINTHIANS 6:9–10 NCV

The acts of the flesh are obvious: sexual immorality, impurity and debauchery; idolatry and witchcraft; hatred, discord, jealousy, fits of rage, selfish ambition, dissensions, factions and envy; drunkenness, orgies, and the like. I warn you, as I did before, that those who live like this will not inherit the kingdom of God.

GALATIANS 5:19–21 NIV

But now I am writing to you not to associate with anyone who bears the name of brother if he is guilty of sexual immorality or greed, or is an idolater, reviler, drunkard, or swindler—not even to eat with such a one.

1 CORINTHIANS 5:11 ESV

For the overseer must be blameless, as God's steward; not self-pleasing, not easily angered, not given to wine, not violent, not greedy for dishonest gain; but given to hospitality, a lover of good, sober minded, fair, holy, self-controlled.

TITUS 1:7–8 WEB

Do not get drunk with wine, which will only ruin you; instead, be filled with the Spirit.

EPHESIANS 5:18 GNT

Those who stay long at the wine; those who go to seek out mixed wine. Don't look at the wine when it is red, when it sparkles in the cup, when it goes down smoothly. In the end, it bites like a snake, and poisons like a viper. Your eyes will see strange things, and your mind will imagine confusing things.

PROVERBS 23:30–33 WEB

Wine is a mocker, and beer is a brawler. Whoever is led astray by them is not wise.
PROVERBS 20:1 WEB

Let us live and conduct ourselves honorably and becomingly as in the [open light of] day, not in reveling (carousing) and drunkenness, not in immorality and debauchery (sensuality and licentiousness), not in quarreling and jealousy.

ROMANS 13:13 AMPC

"You are filled with shame instead of glory. You also— drink! And be exposed as uncircumcised! The cup of the LORD's right hand *will be* turned against you, and utter shame will be on your glory."

HABAKKUK 2:16 NKJV

ANGELS

APP: *Angel mania has flooded popular culture. There are angel-only boutiques, seminars, and newsletters. There are even workshops you can attend to learn how to unleash your "inner angel." For some people, angels offer a type of spirituality that doesn't involve any commitment to God. Others think angels are a way to get help without asking God directly—especially with those who feel the need to have a guardian angel for protection. But most of the interest in angels is based on faulty information.*

The Bible is the best place to learn about angels. Since God created them, He's the one who can tell us what we need to know. It's good for us to be aware that God does provide angelic protection for us. Knowing this should help us to be less fearful of our situation and our enemies. Imagine how different our lives could be if we understood more about the way God uses angels to protect us.

Be encouraged that angels are closer than you think, and there are millions of them on hand at God's command to help us deal with the issues of life—whether at home, school, or wherever you may be.

And suddenly there was with the angel a multitude of the heavenly host, praising God and saying, "Glory to God in the highest heaven, and on earth peace among those whom he favors!"

LUKE 2:13–14 NRSV

But to which of the angels has He ever said: "Sit at My right hand, till I make Your enemies Your footstool"? Are they not all ministering spirits sent forth to minister for those who will inherit salvation?

HEBREWS 1:13–14 NKJV

**Do not neglect to show hospitality
to strangers, for thereby some have
entertained angels unawares.**
HEBREWS 13:2 ESV

Bless the LORD, O you his angels, you mighty ones who do his bidding, obedient to his spoken word.

PSALM 103:20 NRSV

"But about that day or hour no one knows, neither the angels in heaven, nor the Son, but only the Father."

MARK 13:32 NRSV

God did not spare the angels who sinned, but threw them into hell, where they are kept chained in darkness, waiting for the Day of Judgment.

2 PETER 2:4 GNT

ANGER

APP: *We were interviewing people for a film project at a mall in Southern California. I approached a guy who made me feel small because he was so big. Holding the microphone in front of his face, I asked him a question. He pushed his hat back and said, "I don't like it when people ask me that kind of question. It makes me angry." He proceeded to pound his right fist into his left hand. I don't like to be around angry people—especially if I think they might do harm to my body! Of course there are times when I don't even want to be around myself when I get angry.*

So many people don't know how to handle anger. Sometimes they bring guns or other weapons to school to deal with their anger. Some allow their anger to flare up at home, and it results in physical violence. Left unchecked, anger can be destructive. But the Bible does say that God gets angry about certain things, and there are times when it's okay to be angry. If you're struggling with an anger problem, ask God to help you.

"In your anger do not sin": Do not let the sun go down while you are still angry, and do not give the devil a foothold.

EPHESIANS 4:26–27 NIV

Everyone should be quick to listen, slow to speak, and should not get angry easily. An angry person doesn't do what God approves of.
JAMES 1:19–20 GWT

Let all bitterness and wrath and anger and clamor and slander be put away from you, with all malice, and be kind to one another, tender hearted, forgiving one another, as God in Christ forgave you.

EPHESIANS 4:31–32 RSV

A quick-tempered man acts foolishly, and a man of evil devices is hated.

PROVERBS 14:17 NASB

Patience is better than strength. Controlling your temper is better than capturing a city.

PROVERBS 16:32 NCV

The LORD is slow to get angry, but his power is great, and he never lets the guilty go unpunished. He displays his power in the whirlwind and the storm. The billowing clouds are the dust beneath his feet.

NAHUM 1:3 NLT

BAD HABITS

APP: *I hate to admit it, but I have a few bad habits
. . .though they're probably not ones you would
notice easily. A few habits I'd like to get rid of, but
I won't bore you with a list. I know I'm not alone in
this struggle. Most everyone has at least one bad
habit they need to kick. Some are more serious than
others. Take, for example, procrastination versus
lying. Or how about always leaving your room a
mess versus gossiping about your friends? Some bad
habits annoy family members and friends. And the
secret habits can be frustrating to us.*

*I get frustrated when I can't seem to kick a bad
habit once and for all. It tends to keep creeping
back. That's when I'm reminded that I don't have the
wisdom or power to break that pattern in my life. I
need God's help. He is the only One who can give
us the strength and guidance necessary for lasting
change in our lives. But we need to be willing to take
Him and the Bible seriously.*

Praise the Lord, my soul, and forget not all his benefits—who forgives all your sins and heals all your diseases, who redeems your life from the pit and crowns you with love and compassion, who satisfies your desires with good things so that your youth is renewed like the eagle's.

Psalm 103:2–5 NIV

Happy are those who don't listen to the wicked, who don't go where sinners go, who don't do what evil people do.

Psalm 1:1 NCV

When you do things, do not let selfishness or pride be your guide. Instead, be humble and give more honor to others than to yourselves.

Philippians 2:3 NCV

In my trouble I called to the Lord; I called to my God for help. In his temple he heard my voice; he listened to my cry for help.

Psalm 18:6 GNT

Blessed is the man who remains steadfast under trial, for when he has stood the test he will receive the crown of life, which God has promised to those who love him.

James 1:12 ESV

Do not be so deceived and misled! Evil companionships (communion, associations) corrupt and deprave good manners and morals and character.

1 Corinthians 15:33 AMPC

BELIEF

APP: *Living in a world lacking absolutes makes it tough to know who and what we can trust. Life can be pretty shaky when it comes to things like relationships, the economy, and the future. And it's also confusing trying to make sense out of life when there seems to be no truth or right and wrong. People are basically doing whatever they've decided is right and convenient for them. I hear celebrities talking about their beliefs, but it's hard to know exactly what it is they do believe in. Yet other people blindly follow them because they appear to be living happy and successful lives.*

If we are going to experience life the way God designed it—in spite of living in this crazy world— we're going to need solid beliefs based on God's unchanging Word. By putting our trust in Jesus, we can be clear on what we believe and have accepted as true. This will give us confidence in daily life. It's worth the time and effort to develop a biblically based set of beliefs. Take time to study God's Word to accurately know what you believe.

Without faith it is impossible to please God, because anyone who comes to him must believe that he exists and that he rewards those who earnestly seek him.

HEBREWS 11:6 NIV

But these have been recorded in order that you may believe that He is the Christ, the Son of God, and that, through believing, you may have Life through His name.

JOHN 20:31 WNT

There's far more to this life than trusting in Christ. There's also suffering for him. And the suffering is as much a gift as the trusting.

PHILIPPIANS 1:29 MSG

"For what my Father wants is that all who see the Son and believe in him should have eternal life. And I [Jesus] will raise them to life on the last day."
JOHN 6:40 GNT

So they said, "Believe on the Lord Jesus Christ, and you will be saved, you and your household."

ACTS 16:31 NKJV

"So I tell you, whatever you ask for in prayer, believe that you have received it, and it will be yours."

MARK 11:24 NRSV

I [John] write these things to you who believe in the name of the Son of God so that you may know that you have eternal life.

1 JOHN 5:13 NIV

But Jesus loudly declared, The one who believes in Me does not [only] believe in and trust in and rely on Me, but [in believing in Me he believes] in Him Who sent Me.

JOHN 12:44 AMPC

But those who depend on faith, not on deeds, and who believe in the God who declares the guilty to be innocent, it is this faith that God takes into account in order to put them right with himself.

ROMANS 4:5 GNT

"I am Light that has come into the world so that all who believe in me won't have to stay any longer in the dark."

JOHN 12:46 MSG

BITTERNESS

APP: *I've got a lemon tree in my backyard, and it frequently produces some bright yellow fruit. If I try to eat the lemons by themselves, they're pretty sour. But if I squeeze the juice out of several lemons, put it in a pitcher, add some water and just a little sugar, I've got some cool lemonade. When situations in your life turn sour, do you react with bitterness, or do you turn them into "lemonade"?*

Hurt and disappointment are a part of life. But how you let them affect you is important. You can become angry and hostile. Or you can embrace what lesson there is to learn and become a stronger, better person. That's not to say you don't have a right to be upset and hurt. Some people can be very cruel, and life isn't always fair. But be careful you don't let bitterness become a cancer eating away at your life from the inside. Being bitter or better has a lot to do with attitude and giving those sour situations over to God. Let Him help you overcome what has happened and move on with your life.

Do not be bitter or angry or mad. Never shout angrily or say things to hurt others. Never do anything evil.

EPHESIANS 4:31 NCV

But if you have bitter envy and self-seeking in your hearts, do not boast and lie against the truth.

JAMES 3:14 NKJV

See to it that no one fails to obtain the grace of God; that no "root of bitterness" springs up and causes trouble, and by it many become defiled.

HEBREWS 12:15 ESV

For if you forgive other people when they sin against you, your heavenly Father will also forgive you. But if you do not forgive others their sins, your Father will not forgive your sins.
MATTHEW 6:14–15 NIV

Don't say, "I will get even for this wrong." Wait for the LORD to handle the matter.

PROVERBS 20:22 NLT

Hate stirs up trouble, but love forgives all offenses.

PROVERBS 10:12 GNT

BODY MOD

APP: *I was speaking at an event in New York where I met a guy who should be a national spokesman for body mod. To begin with, this guy had dozens of visible tats on his upper body. But what really fascinated me were the piercings he had in his head.*

There were the normal ear studs and a few in his eyebrows, but the one that really got my attention was the metal rod that went straight through the bottom of his nose. It was chrome, about six inches long, and as big around as a pencil. Each tip was sharp and had been bent around so they pointed forward. And last but not least was the car antenna attached to this guy's left shoulder. I never did figure out what it was for. He was an amazing piece of work!

Body mod is popular. It's a way to express yourself in an artsy sort of way. It seems like nearly everyone has an opinion about tats and piercings. But what does God have to say about it? He's really the only One who matters. Our bodies belong to Him, so it's important to get His take on things like body mod.

Or do you not know that your body is the temple
of the Holy Spirit *who is* in you, whom you have
from God, and you are not your own? For you were
bought at a price; therefore glorify God in your body
and in your spirit, which are God's.

1 CORINTHIANS 6:19–20 NKJV

See, I have engraved you on the palms of my hands;
your walls are ever before me.

ISAIAH 49:16 NIV

Don't you know that you are God's temple and that
God's Spirit lives in you? If anyone destroys God's
temple, God will destroy him because God's temple is
holy. You are that holy temple!

1 CORINTHIANS 3:16–17 GWT

From now on, let no one cause me any trouble, for
I bear the marks of the Lord Jesus branded on my
body.

GALATIANS 6:17 WEB

And you are not your own, for you have been
redeemed at infinite cost. Therefore glorify God in
your bodies.

1 CORINTHIANS 6:20 WNT

It shall be as a sign to you upon your hand and as
a memorial between your eyes, that the law of the
Lord may be in your mouth; for with a strong hand
the Lord has brought you out of Egypt.

EXODUS 13:9 AMPC

BULLYING

APP: *A teen girl was crying as she told her school counselor that she couldn't possibly go to class. The night before, a classmate had posted a video on YouTube with a group of other students bad-mouthing her, calling her "spoiled," a "brat," and a "slut." The girl also told her counselor that text messages had been flying, and half the school had probably seen the video. She was a victim of cyber-bullying.*

Whether it happens in cyberspace or face-to-face, bullying is always cruel and hurtful. Some students have been traumatized so much that they felt the only way out was suicide. It's too bad we can't learn to celebrate our differences and stop picking on others.

Even if you've never personally been bullied, there's a good chance you know someone who has been a target. Either way, God has something to say about what to do if you've experienced bullying or how to help someone else who has suffered. You won't find the word bullying in the Bible, but you will find some solid answers for this issue of life. Once you read these verses, ask God how to best apply these truths.

He who says he is in the light, and hates his brother, is in darkness until now.

1 John 2:9 nkjv

Pride only breeds quarrels, but with ones who take advice is wisdom.

Proverbs 13:10 web

A gentle answer will calm a person's anger, but an unkind answer will cause more anger.

Proverbs 15:1 ncv

God has broken the rule of the wicked, the power of the bully-rulers that crushed many people. A relentless rain of cruel outrage established a violent rule of anger rife with torture and persecution.
Isaiah 14:5–6 msg

Those who hate others are murderers, and you know that murderers do not have eternal life in them.

1 John 3:15 gnt

"But the cowardly, the unbelieving, the vile, the murderers, the sexually immoral, those who practice magic arts, the idolaters and all liars—they will be consigned to the fiery lake of burning sulfur. This is the second death."

Revelation 21:8 niv

**"Fear not, therefore; you are of
more value than many sparrows."**
MATTHEW 10:31 ESV

Why do you boast of evil, you mighty hero? Why do
you boast all day long, you who are a disgrace in the
eyes of God?

PSALM 52:1 NIV

God didn't give us a cowardly spirit but a spirit of
power, love, and good judgment.

2 TIMOTHY 1:7 GWT

CHEATING

APP: *How far would you go to win? A high school football coach was suspended because he moved a marker on the field so his team could win the game. A friend asks you to text answers to a test. Is it ever okay to cheat and be dishonest?*

The popular thinking of today makes it acceptable to do whatever you think is right to get the results you desire. The problem is, the more we cheat and don't get caught, the more temptation there is to keep on deceiving. But sooner or later it's gonna catch up to us. It all starts in the little things that gradually evolve into bigger schemes.

Cheating not only affects whomever we're deceiving; it affects our relationships with others. Friends and family begin wondering if they can trust us. We end up living a lie and deceiving ourselves. Cheating is a hard habit to break, but it can be done. It starts by a willingness to want to live honestly and then recognizing that we need God's help to change.

Dishonest scales *are* an abomination to the Lord, but a just weight *is* His delight.

Proverbs 11:1 nkjv

What shall I say about the homes of the wicked filled with treasures gained by cheating? What about the disgusting practice of measuring out grain with dishonest measures? How can I tolerate your merchants who use dishonest scales and weights?
Micah 6:10–11 nlt

Doomed is the one who builds his house by injustice and enlarges it by dishonesty; who makes his people work for nothing and does not pay their wages.

Jeremiah 22:13 gnt

Bread gained by deceit is sweet, but afterward the mouth will be full of gravel.

Proverbs 20:17 nrsv

"Don't exploit your friend or rob him. Don't hold back the wages of a hired hand overnight."

Leviticus 19:13 msg

CHOICES / DECISIONS

APP: *Cell phones are a must-have item. Without them, we'd be lost. I overheard a girl talking with her friends say, "How did people ever survive without cell phones?" They did, but it's hardly an option anymore. Think about the selections we can choose from when it comes to technology. There are hundreds of handsets available and even more apps, depending on your equipment. I can only imagine the choices that will be accessible in the future. It makes my brain hurt!*

Every day we make dozens of choices. How we choose to live today will determine how we live tomorrow. We're products today of the choices we've made in the past. And our future's being directly affected by the choices we're making right now. What kind of choices are you making? Are you happy with the results? It's all about learning to choose what's best instead of just settling for whatever seems easy at the time. Using God's Word as a filter can help us make better choices. But it's going to take time to learn what the Bible teaches and how to apply it to our lives.

"And if you be unwilling to serve the Lord, choose this day whom you will serve, whether the gods your fathers served in the region beyond the River, or the gods of the Amorites in whose land you dwell; but as for me and my house, we will serve the Lord."

Joshua 24:15 rsv

The human mind plans the way, but the Lord directs the steps.

Proverbs 16:9 nrsv

"But only God has wisdom and power, good advice and understanding."
Job 12:13 ncv

Trust in the Lord with all your heart and do not lean on your own understanding. In all your ways acknowledge Him, and He will make your paths straight.

Proverbs 3:5–6 nasb

Your word is a lamp for my feet and a light for my path.

Psalm 119:105 gwt

COMPASSION

APP: *A four-year-old boy lived next door to an elderly man who had recently lost his wife. When he saw his neighbor cry, the little boy went into the man's yard, climbed onto his lap, and just sat there. When his mother asked what he had said to the man, the little boy simply replied, "Nothing. I just helped him cry." That's compassion. It's more than just sympathy or concern. It's putting our caring into action. It's one thing to see someone hurting or hungry or lonely, but it's another story to actually do something about it.*

When was the last time you helped someone cry? There are a lot of hurting people in our world today who would love to have someone quietly understand and cry with them. (Guys, this goes for you too!) We don't have to look very far to find someone whose life has been slammed and needs to experience our kindness. These people are on our campuses, in our neighborhoods, at work, and sometimes even in our own homes. Or maybe it's a child living in a foreign land who doesn't have clothes to wear or enough to eat. Let's work together, caring for the problems of others as if they were our own.

"A new commandment I give you, to love one another; that as I have loved you, you also may love one another. It is by this that every one will know that you are my disciples—if you love one another."

JOHN 13:34–35 WNT

And become useful *and* helpful *and* kind to one another, tenderhearted (compassionate, understanding, loving-hearted), forgiving one another [readily and freely], as God in Christ forgave you.

EPHESIANS 4:32 AMPC

The Lord's love never ends;
his mercies never stop.
LAMENTATIONS 3:22 NCV

Finally, all of you should be of one mind. Sympathize with each other. Love each other as brothers and sisters. Be tenderhearted, and keep a humble attitude.

1 PETER 3:8 NLT

He will again have compassion on us; He will subdue *and* tread underfoot our iniquities. You will cast all *our* sins into the depths of the sea.

MICAH 7:19 AMPC

"This is what the LORD All-Powerful says: 'Do what is right and true. Be kind and merciful to each other.'"

ZECHARIAH 7:9 NCV

CONSEQUENCES

APP: *I've lost track of the number of high school students who've told me that they didn't know there were consequences for their choices. Huh? It doesn't take a rocket scientist to figure out how they reached their conclusion. Popular thinking tells us that we don't have to be concerned about any outcome for our decisions. It's pretty appealing to think we can do anything we want and not worry about the consequences. But it's an ugly lie to live by.*

Every choice—no matter how insignificant it may seem—has a consequence. One small decision can change the entire history of our lives. The problem is that our culture says there are no consequences. I think deep inside we all know this isn't true, but it tends to make life less complex. Consequences can change our lives for the good or the bad. Each time we are faced with a decision, we should think about the cost: If I make this decision today, what will it cost me tomorrow? Next week? Next year? If we learn to make better choices, the consequences will be more positive, and so will our lives.

But Peter and the apostles answered and said, We must obey God rather than men.

ACTS 5:29 ASV

The prudent sees danger and hides himself, but the simple go on and suffer for it.

PROVERBS 22:3 ESV

**Do not be deceived: God cannot be mocked.
A man reaps what he sows.**
GALATIANS 6:7 NIV

Say to the people of Israel: Those who curse their God will be punished for their sin.

LEVITICUS 24:15 NLT

For all who eat and drink without discerning the body, eat and drink judgment against themselves.

1 CORINTHIANS 11:29 NRSV

CREATION

APP: *Visiting the San Antonio Zoo was an awesome adventure. Lions, tigers, bears, and monkeys in environments that resembled their natural habitats. The aquarium was filled with dozens of fish in different shapes, sizes, and colors. Right next door, the reptile building contained almost every kind of snake and lizard you could possibly imagine. There were cages where you could actually walk among birds and butterflies. And I can't leave out the big dudes—giraffes, rhinos, and elephants. All amazing animals with fascinating capabilities and unbelievable strength.*

Walking through the zoo, I wondered how someone could really believe in evolution. How can you observe all these creatures with their unique features, colors, and abilities and truly believe they're all a result of some random mutations over the span of millions of years? To me, it makes more sense to enjoy creation and give the credit to the Creator. We may not be able to understand or explain how God created everything in the universe, but that doesn't mean it isn't true.

In the beginning God created the heavens and the earth. The earth was without form and void, and darkness was upon the face of the deep; and the Spirit of God was moving over the face of the waters. And God said, "Let there be light"; and there was light. And God saw that the light was good; and God separated the light from the darkness. God called the light Day, and the darkness he called Night. And there was evening and there was morning, one day.

GENESIS 1:1–5 RSV

And God said, Let there be a firmament in the midst of the waters, and let it divide the waters from the waters. And God made the firmament, and divided the waters which were under the firmament from the waters which were above the firmament: and it was so. And God called the firmament Heaven. And there was evening and there was morning, a second day.

GENESIS 1:6–8 ASV

Then God said, "Let the waters under the heavens be gathered together into one place, and let the dry *land* appear"; and it was so. And God called the dry *land* Earth, and the gathering together of the waters He called Seas. And God saw that *it was* good. Then God said, "Let the earth bring forth grass, the herb *that* yields seed, *and* the fruit tree *that* yields fruit according to its kind, whose seed *is* in itself, on the earth"; and it was so. And the earth brought forth grass, the herb *that* yields seed according to its kind, and the tree *that* yields fruit, whose seed *is* in itself according to its kind. And God saw that *it was* good. So the evening and the morning were the third day.

GENESIS 1:9–13 NKJV

And God saw every thing that he had made, and behold, it was very good. And the evening and the morning were the sixth day.

GENESIS 1:31 WBT

For you shall go out in joy, and be led back in peace; the mountains and the hills before you shall burst into song, and all the trees of the field shall clap their hands.

ISAIAH 55:12 NRSV

Even before he made the world, God loved us and chose us in Christ to be holy and without fault in his eyes.

EPHESIANS 1:4 NLT

Then God said, "Let us make human beings in our image and likeness. And let them rule over the fish in the sea and the birds in the sky, over the tame animals, over all the earth, and over all the small crawling animals on the earth." So God created human beings in his image. In the image of God he created them. He created them male and female. God blessed them and said, "Have many children and grow in number. Fill the earth and be its master. Rule over the fish in the sea and over the birds in the sky and over every living thing that moves on the earth."

GENESIS 1:26–28 NCV

CROSS / CRUCIFIXION

APP: *Crosses have been making a fashion statement for quite some time. Even celebs wear them on necklaces, earrings, and bracelets. Some people wear shirts adorned with crosses or choose to have a cross tattooed somewhere on their bodies. It all seems kind of strange when you consider how crosses have been used throughout human history—and still are in some parts of the world.*

In Jesus' time, crosses were a form of execution used by the Romans—much like lethal injection or the electric chair are used today. Historians say crucifixion was one of the most painful ways ever devised for a person to die. Crucifixion was the way Jesus died. But His death was not ordinary; neither did He do anything to deserve a criminal's death. The cross expresses the depth of our sin, but it also shows us the unconditional love of God. It is the only way to receive forgiveness for our sins and experience eternal life.

What's your attitude toward the cross? Maybe you don't care all that much about what Jesus did for you when He was crucified. Some people are skeptical about the whole thing. Others believe and are forever changed.

Carrying his own cross, Jesus went out to a place called The Place of the Skull, which in the Hebrew language is called Golgotha.

JOHN 19:17 NCV

"You and all the people of Israel must understand that this man stands in your presence with a healthy body because of the power of Jesus Christ from Nazareth. You crucified Jesus Christ, but God has brought him back to life."

ACTS 4:10 GWT

"They will then hand him over to the Romans for mockery and torture and crucifixion. On the third day he will be raised up alive."

MATTHEW 20:19 MSG

Jesus said to her, "I am the resurrection and the life. He who believes in me will still live, even if he dies."

JOHN 11:25 WEB

It was also Christ's purpose to end the hatred between the two groups, to make them into one body, and to bring them back to God. Christ did all this with his death on the cross.

EPHESIANS 2:16 NCV

With great power the apostles continued to testify to the resurrection of the Lord Jesus. And God's grace was so powerfully at work in them all.

ACTS 4:33 NIV

CULTS

APP: *A lot of strange spirituality is happening today. People are searching for spiritual answers to life. But often they don't want to accept the simple truth of Jesus' teaching, so they look in other places. Some people turn to extreme religions filled with lies and false teaching. These cults are often under the direction of a captivating leader who deceives and manipulates people into following him. These cults—or false religions—come in all shapes and sizes. There's something out there that will appeal to almost anyone. Some of the newer cults have become like spiritual buffets, taking bits of different religions that have just a pinch of truth so they seem legit.*

Cults take people down a path that leads them away from Jesus and the truth. One sure way to find out if a brand of spirituality is a cult is to look at who they say Jesus is and how they view the Bible. It usually doesn't take long before you realize you're dealing with a false religion. That's why it's important for us to know what the Bible teaches and to use it as a filter to separate lies from the truth.

But remember, my friends, what you were told in the past by the apostles of our Lord Jesus Christ. They said to you, "When the last days come, people will appear who will make fun of you, people who follow their own godless desires." These are the people who cause divisions, who are controlled by their natural desires, who do not have the Spirit.

JUDE 1:17–19 GNT

For thus says the LORD of hosts, the God of Israel: Do not let the prophets and the diviners who are among you deceive you, and do not listen to the dreams that they dream, for it is a lie that they are prophesying to you in my name; I did not send them, says the LORD.
JEREMIAH 29:8–9 NRSV

"But a prophet who presumes to speak in my name anything I have not commanded, or a prophet who speaks in the name of other gods, is to be put to death." You may say to yourselves, "How can we know when a message has not been spoken by the LORD?" If what a prophet proclaims in the name of the LORD does not take place or come true, that is a message the LORD has not spoken. That prophet has spoken presumptuously, so do not be alarmed.

DEUTERONOMY 18:20–22 NIV

"False Christs and false prophets will come and perform great wonders and miracles. They will try to fool even the people God has chosen, if that is possible. So be careful. I have warned you about all this before it happens."

MARK 13:22–23 NCV

Dear friends, don't believe all people who say that they have the Spirit. Instead, test them. See whether the spirit they have is from God, because there are many false prophets in the world. This is how you can recognize God's Spirit: Every person who declares that Jesus Christ has come as a human has the Spirit that is from God. But every person who doesn't declare that Jesus Christ has come as a human has a spirit that isn't from God. This is the spirit of the antichrist that you have heard is coming. That spirit is already in the world. Dear children, you belong to God. So you have won the victory over these people, because the one who is in you is greater than the one who is in the world. These people belong to the world. That's why they speak the thoughts of the world, and the world listens to them. We belong to God. The person who knows God listens to us. Whoever doesn't belong to God doesn't listen to us. That's how we can tell the Spirit of truth from the spirit of lies.

1 JOHN 4:1–6 GWT

Do not be led away by diverse and strange teachings; for it is well that the heart be strengthened by grace, not by foods, which have not benefited their adherents.

HEBREWS 13:9 RSV

For the household gods utter nonsense, and the diviners see lies; they tell false dreams and give empty consolation. Therefore the people wander like sheep; they are afflicted for lack of a shepherd.

ZECHARIAH 10:2 ESV

Do not get involved in foolish discussions about spiritual pedigrees or in quarrels and fights about obedience to Jewish laws. These things are useless and a waste of time. If people are causing divisions among you, give a first and second warning. After that, have nothing more to do with them. For people like that have turned away from the truth, and their own sins condemn them.

TITUS 3:9–11 NLT

CUTTING

APP: *Megan was in the audience at one of my school assemblies. After my presentation at her high school, she patiently waited off to the side as I talked with other students. Once everyone else had pretty much left the gym, she made her way over to me. "Look, Steve," Megan said as she turned her arms over to reveal her cut wrists to me.*

"Give me a good reason to stop."

"Because it doesn't solve anything," I responded.

"I know," Megan said. "But at least I can be numb for a while and not deal with the pain in my life."

Cutting and self-mutilation have become a huge issue with teen girls and guys. It's because of the hurt and not knowing how to handle it. Kids frequently tell me that if they cut themselves, the pain on the inside doesn't hurt so badly. When life hurts really badly, we need to find a way to handle the agony. Close friends can be a great source of encouragement. But lasting strength and hope can only come from Jesus. He understands our situation and has the ability to carry us through the storms of life.

Let me hear joy and gladness; let the bones you have crushed rejoice. Hide your face from my sins and blot out all my iniquity. Create in me a pure heart, O God, and renew a steadfast spirit within me. Do not cast me from your presence or take your Holy Spirit from me. Restore to me the joy of your salvation and grant me a willing spirit, to sustain me.

PSALM 51:8–12 NIV

Or do you not know that your bodies are a sanctuary of the Holy Spirit who is within you—the Spirit whom you have from God?

1 CORINTHIANS 6:19 WNT

Casting the whole of your care [all your anxieties, all your worries, all your concerns, once and for all] on Him, for He cares for you affectionately *and* cares about you watchfully.
1 PETER 5:7 AMPC

"You shall not make any cuts in your body for the dead. . . . I am the LORD."

LEVITICUS 19:28 NASB

Obey the LORD and you will live a long life, content and safe from harm.

PROVERBS 19:23 GNT

"But nothing is impossible for God."
LUKE 1:37 GWT

"I know what I'm doing. I have it all planned out—plans to take care of you, not abandon you, plans to give you the future you hope for."

JEREMIAH 29:11 MSG

DATING

APP: *My friend and I wanted to double-date and attend a concert at an arena about forty-five minutes from our house. It ended up being one of the worst dates of my life. We had one slight problem—neither of us had a driver's license.*

My mom volunteered to drive us and get our tickets. But she conveniently forgot to tell us she also bought a ticket for herself! (Hang on, it gets worse!) She sat between the two girls during the entire show. We hardly talked with our dates because they were so busy chatting with my mom! Believe me, I don't recommend this arrangement for anyone. Fortunately, my dating life did improve and I learned a valuable lesson: Leave Mom at home!

Dating can occupy a huge part of a teen's life. And even though the Bible doesn't use the word dating, God has plenty to say about this area of life. There's no doubt He wants us to have fun. But God wants us to do it in such a way that we respect the person we're going out with and please Him in the process.

Love must be sincere. Hate what is evil; cling to what is good. Be devoted to one another in love. Honor one another above yourselves.

Romans 12:9–10 NIV

Flee the evil desires of youth and pursue righteousness, faith, love, and peace, along with those who call on the Lord out of a pure heart.

2 Timothy 2:22 NIV

Flee from sexual immorality. All other sins a person commits are outside the body, but whoever sins sexually, sins against their own body.

1 Corinthians 6:18 NIV

Flee also youthful lusts; but pursue righteousness, faith, love, peace with those who call on the Lord out of a pure heart.

2 Timothy 2:22 NKJV

Don't allow love to turn into lust, setting off a downhill slide into sexual promiscuity, filthy practices, or bullying greed.

Ephesians 5:3 MSG

Put to death, therefore, whatever belongs to your earthly nature: sexual immorality, impurity, lust, evil desires and greed, which is idolatry.

Colossians 3:5 NIV

Keep *and* guard your heart with all vigilance *and* above all that you guard, for out of it flow the springs of life.

Proverbs 4:23 AMPC

Do not be deceived: "Bad company ruins good morals."

1 CORINTHIANS 15:33 RSV

Do not be unequally yoked with unbelievers.
For what partnership has righteousness with
lawlessness? Or what fellowship has light with
darkness? What accord has Christ with Belial?
Or what portion does a believer share
with an unbeliever?

2 CORINTHIANS 6:14–15 ESV

Guard your heart above all else, for it determines the
course of your life.

PROVERBS 4:23 NLT

DEATH / DYING

APP: *Death isn't something we like to talk about—especially when we're young. We have our whole lives ahead of us, so who wants to talk about dying? Then reality hits the first time we lose a relative or close friend. Memories flood our hearts and minds. There's an empty place at the table. The calls and text messages suddenly stop. There's a pain deep in the pit of our stomach as we ache to have this special person back again. It's even worse if the death was sudden or we weren't sure where the person was spiritually. Sometimes we scream out to God, demanding to know why. But it's not for us to know this side of eternity.*

Dying and death are never easy topics to talk about, but they're a part of life. God does offer some advice on how to deal with this painful experience. It can be difficult to process, especially while we're grieving. That's why good friends can be so important to us during tough times like these. You may not need God's advice on this subject now, but sooner or later you will—for you or a friend.

We are confident and prefer to live away from this body and to live with the Lord.

2 Corinthians 5:8 gwt

Even when the way goes through Death Valley, I'm not afraid when you walk at my side. Your trusty shepherd's crook makes me feel secure.

Psalm 23:4 msg

"Blessed are those who mourn, for they shall be comforted."

Matthew 5:4 nasb

"O death, where is your victory? O death, where is your sting?" For sin is the sting that results in death, and the law gives sin its power.

1 Corinthians 15:55–56 nlt

Lord, have mercy on me. See how my enemies torment me. Snatch me back from the jaws of death.

Psalm 9:13 nlt

You have rescued me from death and kept me from defeat. And so I walk in the presence of God, in the light that shines on the living.

Psalm 56:13 gnt

Treasures of wickedness profit nothing, but righteousness (moral and spiritual rectitude in every area and relation) delivers from death.

Proverbs 10:2 ampc

The teaching of the wise is a fountain of life, that one may avoid the snares of death.

Proverbs 13:14 rsv

"Very truly, I tell you, anyone who hears my word and believes him who sent me has eternal life, and does not come under judgment, but has passed from death to life."

JOHN 5:24 NRSV

So you see, just as death came into the world through a man, now the resurrection from the dead has begun through another man.
1 CORINTHIANS 15:21 NLT

[God] Who delivered us from so great a death, and does deliver us; in whom we trust that He will still deliver *us*.

2 CORINTHIANS 1:10 NKJV

"He will wipe every tear from their eyes. There won't be any more death. There won't be any grief, crying, or pain, because the first things have disappeared."

REVELATION 21:4 GWT

DEMONS

APP: *Demons are more than just figures of speech, cosmic forces, or concepts that merely exist in our minds. They are real spirit beings; but they are not able to be everywhere at once, although they are not as restricted as humans by the normal barriers of space. Demons possess intelligence, emotions, wills, and even personalities. They can also possess superhuman strength at given times. Demons are angels who chose to join the devil's rebellion against God and continue to oppose His purposes and work here in this world.*

Both the Bible and Jesus confirm the reality of demons. Numerous times during His earthly ministry, Jesus encountered them. We battle against demons in the spiritual realm just as we battle against the devil. All but one book in the New Testament—Hebrews—mentions them. But just like the devil, demons are a defeated enemy because of what Jesus did on the cross. With Jesus' help we can win the battle against the demonic forces that oppose God's work in our lives. If we don't want to be defeated, we need to rely on the strength of the Lord and the truth of His Word.

And angels who did not keep (care for, guard, and hold to) their own first place of power but abandoned their proper dwelling place—these He has reserved in custody in eternal chains (bonds) under the thick gloom of utter darkness until the judgment *and* doom of the great day.

JUDE 1:6 AMPC

The huge dragon was thrown out—that ancient serpent, named the Devil, or Satan, that deceived the whole world. He was thrown down to earth, and all his angels with him.

REVELATION 12:9 GNT

Moreover, demons came out of many people, shouting, "You are the Son of God!" But he rebuked them and would not allow them to speak, because they knew he was the Messiah.

LUKE 4:41 NIV

"These are some of the signs that will accompany believers: They will throw out demons in my name, they will speak in new tongues."
MARK 16:17 MSG

For I am convinced that neither death nor life, neither angels nor demons, neither the present nor the future . . .will be able to separate us from the love of God.

ROMANS 8:38–39 NIV

DEPRESSION

APP: *Sad feelings of gloom can be caused by lots of different things. Depression can be brought on by never-ending boredom or a chemical imbalance that causes your mind and emotions to get messed up. A low mood can also be caused by a significant life event like the death of someone you love or your parents getting a divorce. You can feel depressed because of stress, low self-esteem, and even family history. Maybe a close relative has also struggled with feelings of inadequacy and dreariness. Beating depression starts by defining it—what's causing you to have these feelings. But we also have to remember that there are times when we will feel down just because it's a normal part of life. Maybe our depression is caused by being tired or stressed out because of real-life stuff happening. Even some people in the Bible struggled with depression. We are not alone if we have battled depression. The cool thing is that God doesn't leave us on our own. He has some answers in His Word that can help and encourage us. It may take some time, but with God's help we can leave the gloominess behind.*

We are hard pressed on every side, but not crushed; perplexed, but not in despair; persecuted, but not abandoned; struck down, but not destroyed.

2 CORINTHIANS 4:8–9 NIV

Is anyone crying for help? GOD is listening, ready to rescue you.

PSALM 34:17 MSG

"When you pass through the waters I will be with you; and through the rivers, they shall not overwhelm you; when you walk through fire you shall not be burned, and the flame shall not consume you."

ISAIAH 43:2 RSV

Fear not [there is nothing to fear], for I am with you; do not look around you in terror *and* be dismayed, for I am your God. I will strengthen *and* harden you to difficulties, yes, I will help you; yes, I will hold you up *and* retain you with My [victorious] right hand of rightness *and* justice.
ISAIAH 41:10 AMPC

Humble yourselves therefore under the mighty hand of God, that he may exalt you in due time; casting all your anxiety upon him, because he careth for you.

1 PETER 5:6–7 ASV

Praise be to the God and Father of our Lord Jesus Christ, the Father of compassion and the God of all comfort, who comforts us in all our troubles, so that we can comfort those in any trouble with the comfort we ourselves receive from God.

2 CORINTHIANS 1:3–4 NIV

**He heals the brokenhearted,
and binds up their wounds.**
PSALM 147:3 RSV

Those who love your law have perfect security, and there is nothing that can make them fall.

PSALM 119:165 GNT

For I am persuaded beyond doubt (am sure) that neither death nor life, nor angels nor principalities, nor things impending *and* threatening nor things to come, nor powers, nor height nor depth, nor anything else in all creation will be able to separate us from the love of God which is in Christ Jesus our Lord.

ROMANS 8:38–39 AMPC

DEVIL / SATAN

APP: *Satan has done an amazing job to confuse us about his real identity. Lots of movies, TV shows, video games, music, and Web sites characterize him as something totally different from reality. Satan is portrayed as everything from a clownlike buffoon to a hideous part-animal/alien monster. He is a brilliant strategist whose arsenal of weapons includes everything from false teaching to distractions. This just makes us all the more vulnerable to his deception and tricks. No wonder so many people don't take him seriously today.*

If you don't believe that your enemy is real, then you won't worry about being attacked. Satan's goal is to confuse and disarm us. That's why it's so important to understand what's going on from a biblical worldview. We need to know what the Bible teaches about the devil so we have an accurate picture of his true character. It's important not to underestimate him, but we also need to remember that he is a mortally wounded foe. God's Word is the ultimate source of truth and a vital weapon against Satan.

Be alert, be on watch! Your enemy, the Devil, roams around like a roaring lion, looking for someone to devour. Be firm in your faith and resist him, because you know that other believers in all the world are going through the same kind of sufferings.

1 Peter 5:8–9 gnt

Submit therefore to God: resist the Devil, and he will flee from you.

James 4:7 wnt

"The thief comes only to steal and kill and destroy; I [Jesus] came that they may have life, and have *it* abundantly."

John 10:10 nasb

Then Jesus said to him, Begone, Satan! For it has been written, You shall worship the Lord your God, and Him alone shall you serve.

Matthew 4:10 ampc

Whoever continues to sin belongs to the Devil, because the Devil has sinned from the very beginning. The Son of God appeared for this very reason, to destroy what the Devil had done.

1 John 3:8 gnt

[God] has delivered us from the power of darkness and conveyed *us* into the kingdom of the Son of His love.

Colossians 1:13 nkjv

DIFFICULTIES

APP: *I despise having technical difficulties. You know—when your cell phone keeps dropping calls or iTunes isn't working when you want to download a song. No one likes the frustration of dealing with too much drama from a friend; pressure from parents, teachers, or a boss; or loneliness because you've been cut out of "the group." Life is filled with difficulties—everything from relationships to health to finishing a test, to obstacles that hinder us from achieving our goals. Difficulties can become more than frustrating when they go beyond our ability to grapple with them. We can't avoid difficulties; they're a part of life. But we can change our attitude toward them. How we view the events of our lives will determine their effect on us. Every difficulty is an opportunity for God to work in our lives. Difficulties are a chance for us to build godly character and deepen our faith. It's about developing the right mental attitude so we're prepared when we come across them. We have to learn to become like the shell of an airplane that expands and contracts in response to the pressure of altitude.*

But in every way we show we are servants of God: in accepting many hard things, in troubles, in difficulties, and in great problems.

2 CORINTHIANS 6:4 NCV

Therefore let us not pass judgment on one another any longer, but rather decide never to put a stumbling block or hindrance in the way of a brother.

ROMANS 14:13 ESV

Behold, the LORD's hand is not shortened, that it cannot save; neither his ear heavy, that it cannot hear.

ISAIAH 59:1 WBT

The righteous cry out, and the LORD hears them; he delivers them from all their troubles.
PSALM 34:17 NIV

"Listen now to my voice; I will give you counsel, and God will be with you: Stand before God for the people, so that you may bring the difficulties to God."

EXODUS 18:19 NKJV

So for the sake of Christ, I am well pleased *and* take pleasure in infirmities, insults, hardships, persecutions, perplexities *and* distresses; for when I am weak [in human strength], then am I [truly] strong (able, powerful in divine strength).

2 CORINTHIANS 12:10 AMPC

DIVORCE

APP: *It's ugly when a family breaks up. Lots of times when divorce happens, it's because a spouse decides it's "all about them" and forgets what a family is all about. A divorce is hard on everyone—but especially on the kids. I don't ask students if they've gone through a divorce; instead, I ask them how many they've experienced. It's not unusual to hear them say three or even four. I once met a sixteen-year-old girl who was going through the sixth divorce of a set of parents.*

When our family breaks up, it can make us feel insecure, and sometimes we even end up blaming ourselves for what happened between our parents. Sometimes we are caught in the middle, and that makes it tough emotionally. Surviving a divorce isn't always easy, but it can be done. We start by not blaming ourselves. Whatever the circumstances, remember it's between Mom and Dad. We need to be careful not to take sides and do the best we can to love both of them. Remember to lean on God— and some close friends—for emotional support. And determine with God's help not to let divorce be an option for your future marriage.

"It was also said, 'Whoever divorces his wife, let him give her a certificate of divorce.' But I say to you that everyone who divorces his wife, except on the ground of sexual immorality, makes her commit adultery, and whoever marries a divorced woman commits adultery."

MATTHEW 5:31–32 ESV

And Pharisees came up to him and tested him by asking, "Is it lawful to divorce one's wife for any cause?" He [Jesus] answered, "Have you not read that he who created them from the beginning made them male and female, and said, 'Therefore a man shall leave his father and his mother and hold fast to his wife, and the two shall become one flesh'? So they are no longer two but one flesh. What therefore God has joined together, let not man separate." They said to him, "Why then did Moses command one to give a certificate of divorce and to send her away?" He said to them, "Because of your hardness of heart Moses allowed you to divorce your wives, but from the beginning it was not so. And I say to you: whoever divorces his wife, except for sexual immorality, and marries another, commits adultery."

MATTHEW 19:3–9 ESV

A wife is bound to her husband as long as he lives. But if her husband dies, she is free to be married to whom she wishes, only in the Lord.

1 CORINTHIANS 7:39 ESV

DOUBT

APP: *Our teen years are frequently filled with doubt. We often find ourselves stuck between belief and disbelief. Life stuff causes us to lack confidence and be unsure about things like self-image, relationships, abilities, faith, and even the future. We doubt when we feel inadequate—sometimes as a result of comparing ourselves to others or false standards. Doubt can create trust issues or a kind of paralysis that can cause us to put off doing something good, but is out of our comfort zone. It can weigh us down with fear and dread so we don't pursue and accomplish what we are passionate about.*

Doubt isn't always bad. It can lead us to question when things don't seem right or we don't completely understand. Doubt can also tell a friend that we care enough to find out what's really going on in their lives when they tell us "everything's cool. . .you don't have to worry about me." Sometimes doubt can help us to deepen our faith as we search for answers to the questions we can't seem to let go of. Doubt can be healthy if it motivates us to search for the truth.

But when you ask him, be sure that your faith is in God alone. Do not waver, for a person with divided loyalty is as unsettled as a wave of the sea that is blown and tossed by the wind.

JAMES 1:6 NLT

I desire therefore that in every place men should pray, without anger *or* quarreling *or* resentment or doubt [in their minds], lifting up holy hands.

1 TIMOTHY 2:8 AMPC

"Truly I tell you, if anyone says to this mountain, 'Go, throw yourself into the sea,' and does not doubt in their heart but believes that what they say will happen, it will be done for them."

MARK 11:23 NIV

But if you have doubts about whether or not you should eat something, you are sinning if you go ahead and do it. For you are not following your convictions. If you do anything you believe is not right, you are sinning.

ROMANS 14:23 NLT

Thomas said, "My Master! My God!" Jesus said, "So, you believe because you've seen with your own eyes. Even better blessings are in store for those who believe without seeing."

JOHN 20:28–29 MSG

DRUGS

APP: *Drug abuse is an increasing problem. It's costly and dangerous. Regularly we hear about another celeb who died of an accidental drug overdose. Kids at school are using all kinds of things to get high without thinking about the consequences of using their "drug of choice." A fifteen-year-old girl put it this way: "When you take drugs, it's like getting in a car with someone you don't know who will take you down a road you've never been before." Unfortunately, it doesn't appear that campaigns like Just Say No are having a big effect on teen drug abuse. Kids at school are getting high to deal with being bored or stressed out. Other teens get high so they can belong to a group or escape from their problems. Alcohol is the number one drug of choice. Drugs and alcohol seem to provide a temporary relief for a life filled with fear and trouble. We have to stop listening to the lies of our culture that tell us to live for the moment and attempt to fill the inner emptiness. This means learning how to better discern between making decisions that are safe and unsafe. There's no better place to turn than God's Word.*

Who are the people who are always crying the blues? Who do you know who reeks of self-pity? Who keeps getting beat up for no reason at all? Whose eyes are bleary and bloodshot? It's those who spend the night with a bottle, for whom drinking is serious business. Don't judge wine by its label, or its bouquet, or its full-bodied flavor. Judge it rather by the hangover it leaves you with—the splitting headache, the queasy stomach. Do you really prefer seeing double, with your speech all slurred, reeling and seasick, drunk as a sailor? "They hit me," you'll say, "but it didn't hurt; they beat on me, but I didn't feel a thing. When I'm sober enough to manage it, bring me another drink!"

PROVERBS 23: 29–35 MSG

But I say, walk by the Spirit, and you will not gratify the desires of the flesh. For the desires of the flesh are against the Spirit, and the desires of the Spirit are against the flesh, for these are opposed to each other, to keep you from doing the things you want to do. But if you are led by the Spirit, you are not under the law. Now the works of the flesh are evident: sexual immorality, impurity, sensuality, idolatry, sorcery, enmity, strife, jealousy, fits of anger, rivalries, dissensions, divisions, envy, drunkenness, orgies, and things like these. I warn you, as I warned you before, that those who do such things will not inherit the kingdom of God. But the fruit of the Spirit is love, joy, peace, patience, kindness, goodness, faithfulness, gentleness, self-control; against such things there is no law. And those who belong to Christ Jesus have crucified the flesh with its passions and desires.

GALATIANS 5:16–24 ESV

EATING DISORDERS

APP: *An eating disorder happens when someone eats or refuses to eat in order to satisfy an emotional need instead of a physical one. Normal is when someone eats when they feel hungry and stops when they feel satisfied. Eating disorders are a way of coping with the disappointments and pain of life. Those who struggle with these issues see the eating disorder as a way to find some type of comfort and peace in the midst of the confusion in their daily lives. These disorders have different names, such as anorexia, bulimia, or binging. But someone could still have a disorder even without belonging to one of these categories. Eating disorders can be a problem for guys and girls.*

There's no way we can cope with the confusion, disillusionment, and pain of life on our own. We're not wired to be capable of this. We need supernatural help that can only come from the living God. Unfortunately, life is not free from sorrow and setbacks. But we have the resources and power necessary to cope and succeed in life. Eating disorders may not be a problem for you, but God can use you to help a friend find a better way to cope.

Didn't you realize that your body is a sacred place, the place of the Holy Spirit? Don't you see that you can't live however you please, squandering what God paid such a high price for? The physical part of you is not some piece of property belonging to the spiritual part of you. God owns the whole works. So let people see God in and through your body.

1 CORINTHIANS 6:19–20 MSG

What's important in all this is that if you keep a holy day, keep it for *God's* sake; if you eat meat, eat it to the glory of God and thank God for prime rib; if you're a vegetarian, eat vegetables to the glory of God and thank God for broccoli. None of us are permitted to insist on our own way in these matters. It's *God* we are answerable to—all the way from life to death and everything in between—not each other. That's why Jesus lived and died and then lived again: so that he could be our Master across the entire range of life and death, and free us from the petty tyrannies of each other.

ROMANS 14:6–9 MSG

For we are God's masterpiece. He has created us anew in Christ Jesus, so we can do the good things he planned for us long ago.

EPHESIANS 2:10 NLT

"Don't judge by his appearance or height, for I have rejected him. The LORD doesn't see things the way you see them. People judge by outward appearance, but the LORD looks at the heart."

1 SAMUEL 16:7 NLT

ENEMIES

APP: *An enemy can come in many different shapes and sizes. The most common enemies are people. Most of us don't suddenly decide to go out and make enemies. Why would we purposely want to make another person hostile toward us? But unfortunately, adversaries and opponents do show up in our lives from time to time. And no matter what we do or say, they are bent on being antagonistic toward us. We also have to remember that sometimes we can be our own worst enemy by working against ourselves. This can happen because of things like abuse, wrong priorities, or out-of-control ambition. Another enemy who should cause us to be on the alert is Satan. He is by far the most dangerous opponent we will ever face. Once you know who your enemies are, the tough part is knowing how to treat them. Fortunately, we can find guidance and encouragement in God's Word. The hard part is obeying and doing what God says to do.*

If you see your enemy hungry, go buy him lunch; if he's thirsty, bring him a drink. Your generosity will surprise him with goodness, and God will look after you.

PROVERBS 25:21–22 MSG

Wounds from a sincere friend are better than many kisses from an enemy.

PROVERBS 27:6 NLT

"You have heard that it was said, 'Love your neighbor and hate your enemy.' But I [Jesus] tell you, love your enemies and pray for those who persecute you."
MATTHEW 5:43–44 NIV

When the LORD takes pleasure in anyone's way, he causes their enemies to make peace with them.

PROVERBS 16:7 NIV

Rescue me from my enemies, LORD, for I hide myself in you.

PSALM 143:9 NIV

The LORD is with me; I will not be afraid. What can mere mortals do to me? The LORD is with me; he is my helper. I look in triumph on my enemies. It is better to take refuge in the LORD than to trust in humans.

PSALM 118:6–8 NIV

ENVIRONMENT

APP: *It's hard to believe that environmental crises actually started way back at the beginning of human history. Adam and Eve—the first man and woman—lived in an amazing paradise. The Garden of Eden was like heaven on earth. Everything was perfect. And Adam and Eve would have lived there forever had they not disobeyed God. But they were deceived by Satan, who disguised himself as a serpent and convinced them that their way was better than God's.*

Adam and Eve's choice to disobey God affected all of creation, including the environment. Previous generations didn't think anything about "small choices" they made environmentally, like dumping garbage into a stream and polluting it. Now we know that just small amounts of garbage in a large quantity of water can be hazardous to human health. That's why it's so important that we learn choices have consequences; and often our consequences affect other people and future generations. We all have to do our part in "going green" and protecting the environment. The Bible provides us with the "why" and even some specific things we can do to make a difference. We have to make up our minds if we think it's worth the time and effort. Then we can do what God asks us to do.

The earth is the Lord's, and everything in it, the world, and all who live in it; for he founded it on the seas and established it on the waters.

PSALM 24:1–2 NIV

He [God] makes springs pour water into the ravines; it flows between the mountains. They give water to all the beasts of the field; the wild donkeys quench their thirst. The birds of the sky nest by the waters; they sing among the branches. He waters the mountains from his upper chambers; the land is satisfied by the fruit of his work. He makes grass grow for the cattle, and plants for people to cultivate—bringing forth food from the earth.

PSALM 104:10–14 NIV

How many are your works, Lord! In wisdom you made them all; the earth is full of your creatures. There is the sea, vast and spacious, teeming with creatures beyond number—living things both large and small.
PSALM 104:24–25 NIV

"Stop and consider the wonderful miracles of God! Do you know how God controls the storm and causes the lightning to flash from his clouds? Do you understand how he moves the clouds with wonderful perfection and skill?"

JOB 37:14–16 NLT

EQUALITY

APP: *While growing up, I was always concerned about everything being fair and equal. I wanted exactly the same size piece of berry pie that my brother and sister had. But most of the time I tried to grab the biggest piece before they did. On Christmas morning I counted the number of presents we all had under the tree. If there was a difference, I would yell, "It's not fair!" Can you relate?*

Unfortunately, life isn't always fair and there have been some serious struggles for equality in this country. A war divided the nation over the freedom of those who were considered less human because of the color of their skin. A battle for the right of women to vote was fought and won. Later a movement swept the country to give equal access to all people—no matter whether they were black or white.

God is the only One who is truly impartial, just, and fair. We see this from the very beginning of human history when He created us male and female—all equal. Jesus removed all the barriers between us when He died on the cross.

So God created mankind in his own image, in the image of God he created him; male and female he created them.

GENESIS 1:27 NIV

In Christ's family there can be no division into Jew and non-Jew, slave and free, male and female. Among us you are all equal. That is, we are all in a common relationship with Jesus Christ. Also, since you are Christ's family, then you are Abraham's famous "descendant," heirs according to the covenant promises.

GALATIANS 3:28–29 MSG

Of course, I don't mean your giving should make life easy for others and hard for yourselves. I only mean that there should be some equality. Right now you have plenty and can help those who are in need. Later, they will have plenty and can share with you when you need it. In this way, things will be equal. As the Scriptures say, "Those who gathered a lot had nothing left over, and those who gathered only a little had enough."

2 CORINTHIANS 8:13–15 NLT

ETERNITY

APP: *Eternity is a difficult idea to wrap our minds around. How do we begin to understand time without beginning or end? The state of being eternal is hard for our finite, limited minds to grasp. Existing for a limitless amount of time seems weird to think about when we're all about living for the moment. Every one of us will die and then enter into a timeless condition of existence. After death we will spend the rest of time existing in heaven or hell according to God's Word.*

It's mind-boggling to think that we make the decision where we will spend eternity. No doubt this is the most important choice we will ever make. That's why we have to get the best, most reliable source of information we can get our hands on before we make this decision. The Bible is the one and only place we need to look. Think about it—who knows more about eternity than the One who is beyond time and space? The Creator of life on earth and throughout the universe: the living God. The cool thing is that God has made it crystal clear how to obtain eternal life.

"For this is how God loved the world: He gave his one and only Son, so that everyone who believes in him will not perish but have eternal life. God sent his Son into the world not to judge the world, but to save the world through him."

JOHN 3:16–17 NLT

Jesus answered, "Everyone who drinks this water will be thirsty again, but whoever drinks the water I give them will never thirst. Indeed, the water I give them will become in them a spring of water welling up to eternal life."

JOHN 4:13–14 NIV

"I [Jesus] tell you the truth, those who listen to my message and believe in God who sent me have eternal life. They will never be condemned for their sins, but they have already passed from death into life. And I assure you that the time is coming, indeed it's here now, when the dead will hear my voice—the voice of the Son of God. And those who listen will live."

JOHN 5:24–25 NLT

"For my Father's will is that everyone who looks to the Son and believes in him shall have eternal life, and I [Jesus] will raise them up at the last day."

JOHN 6:40 NIV

"For you have given him authority over everyone. He [God] gives eternal life to each one you have given him. And this is the way to have eternal life—to know you, the only true God, and Jesus Christ, the one you sent to earth."

JOHN 17:2–3 NLT

But now that you've found you don't have to listen to sin tell you what to do, and have discovered the delight of listening to God telling you, what a surprise! A whole, healed, put-together life right now, with more and more of life on the way! Work hard for sin your whole life and your pension is death. But God's gift is *real life*, eternal life, delivered by Jesus, our Master.

ROMANS 6:22–23 MSG

Here is a trustworthy saying that deserves full acceptance: Christ Jesus came into the world to save sinners—of whom I am the worst. But for that very reason I was shown mercy so that in me, the worst of sinners, Christ Jesus might display his immense patience as an example for those who would believe in him and receive eternal life.
1 TIMOTHY 1:15–16 NIV

He [God] has made everything beautiful in its time. He has also set eternity in the human heart; yet no one can fathom what God has done from beginning to end.

ECCLESIASTES 3:11 NIV

EUTHANASIA

APP: *In the eighteenth century, writers in England used the word* euthanasia *to mean "good death." It referred to a pleasant way to leave this life quietly and well. But today it has taken on a totally different meaning. Our modern-day culture describes euthanasia as the act of permitting someone to die who is hopelessly sick or injured. It can also be used to refer to the act of painlessly killing a person who is suffering from an incurable illness or disease. This complex issue raises the level of emotions fairly high for those who support euthanasia and those who oppose it.*

The best place to look for answers on how to make sense of what some have called the "easy death" is to ask the Creator of life itself His opinion. The Bible makes it clear that God is the One who gives life, and He takes it away. The best thing we can do is to carefully examine the Bible to see how God looks at and values life. Then we can make a "spiritually informed" decision instead of one that is considered a person's right and "politically correct."

For to me, living means living for Christ, and dying is even better. But if I live, I can do more fruitful work for Christ. So I really don't know which is better. I'm torn between two desires: I long to go and be with Christ, which would be far better for me. But for your sakes, it is better that I continue to live. Knowing this, I am convinced that I will remain alive so I can continue to help all of you grow and experience the joy of your faith. And when I come to you again, you will have even more reason to take pride in Christ Jesus because of what he is doing through me.

PHILIPPIANS 1:21–26 NLT

Therefore we do not lose heart. Though outwardly we are wasting away, yet inwardly we are being renewed day by day. For our light and momentary troubles are achieving for us an eternal glory that far outweighs them all. So we fix our eyes not on what is seen, but on what is unseen, since what is seen is temporary, but what is unseen is eternal.

2 CORINTHIANS 4:16–18 NIV

There's an opportune time to do things, a right time for everything on the earth: A right time for birth and another for death.

ECCLESIASTES 3:1–2 MSG

All the days ordained for me
were written in your [God's] book
before one of them came to be.
PSALM 139:16 NIV

EVIL

APP: *There's confusion over what evil is in our culture today, because everything is relative: There is no right and wrong or moral absolutes. But God's perspective is different. Doing something evil is disobeying God and is harmful because of the consequences people experience. Evil came into being because of the freedom of choice. It was a necessary risk when God allowed people and angelic beings to have free will. He knew there was the possibility that someone would choose to rebel against Him. And that's exactly what Satan did. He is the one behind all the wickedness in the world. We don't completely understand why God allows evil, but we do know that He is able to bring glory to Himself through evil by expressing His undeserved favor and justice.*

We will give in to being tempted by evil every time without God's help. He has the power to overcome Satan and gives us all the resources we need through His Son. If we want to experience victory over evil, we need to stop opening ourselves up to every ungodly value and attitude the world puts in our path—no matter how fascinating they may seem. Instead, be consumed by the all-powerful living God.

Whoever of you loves life and desires to see many good days, keep your tongue from evil and your lips from telling lies. Turn from evil and do good; seek peace and pursue it.

PSALM 34:12–14 NIV

Turn from evil and do good, and you will live in the land forever. For the LORD loves justice, and he will never abandon the godly. He will keep them safe forever, but the children of the wicked will die. The godly will possess the land and will live there forever.

PSALM 37:27–29 NLT

Do not be wise in your own eyes; fear the LORD and shun evil. This will bring health to your body and nourishment to your bones.

PROVERBS 3:7–8 NIV

Take your stand with God's loyal community and live, or chase after phantoms of evil and die. GOD can't stand deceivers, but oh how he relishes integrity.

PROVERBS 11:19–20 MSG

"A good man brings good things out of the good stored up in his heart, and an evil man brings evil things out of the evil stored up in his heart. For the mouth speaks what the heart is full of."

LUKE 6:45 NIV

EVOLUTION

APP: *Evolution is the gradual process of something changing into a different and usually more complex or better form. This process can be applied to the gradual development of many different things.*
For example, through practicing and working out we could evolve into a good musician or athlete. Think about how cell phones have evolved the past few years into amazing devices for collecting and processing a variety of content and information.

Most often we find the word evolution *applied to the gradual development of animals, humans, and plant life over millions of years into what they are today. The idea is that the genetic composition of a population changes during successive generations as a result of natural selection. This is supposed to result in the development of a new species. It's an interesting concept, but if this were true, why haven't there been changes and new species with animals and humans in a long time? It actually takes more faith to believe in evolution than creation. We should start giving the Creator more credit for all He has done. And remember, we don't have to be afraid to use the word* evolution. *What matters is how we apply it.*

God spoke: "Swarm, Ocean, with fish and all sea life! Birds, fly through the sky over Earth!" God created the huge whales, all the swarm of life in the waters, and every kind and species of flying birds. God saw that it was good. God blessed them: "Prosper! Reproduce! Fill Ocean! Birds, reproduce on Earth!" It was evening, it was morning—Day Five. God spoke: "Earth, generate life! Every sort and kind: cattle and reptiles and wild animals—all kinds." And there it was: wild animals of every kind, cattle of all kinds, every sort of reptile and bug. God saw that it was good. God spoke: "Let us make human beings in our image, make them reflecting our nature so they can be responsible for the fish in the sea, the birds in the air, the cattle, and, yes, Earth itself, and every animal that moves on the face of Earth." God created human beings; he created them godlike, reflecting God's nature. He created them male and female. God blessed them: "Prosper! Reproduce! Fill Earth! Take charge! Be responsible for fish in the sea and birds in the air, for every living thing that moves on the face of Earth."

GENESIS 1:20–28 MSG

Above all, you must understand that in the last days scoffers will come, scoffing and following their own evil desires. They will say, "Where is this 'coming' he promised? Ever since our ancestors died, everything goes on as it has since the beginning of creation." But they deliberately forget that long ago by God's word the heavens came into being and the earth was formed out of water and by water. By these waters also the world of that time was deluged and destroyed. By the same word the present heavens and earth are reserved for fire, being kept for the day of judgment and destruction of the ungodly.

2 PETER 3:3–7 NIV

FAILURE

APP: *I had to take a speech class when I was a freshman in college. About halfway through the course, the professor asked me to stay after class one day. "Mr. Russo," she said. "Let me encourage you to do yourself and the world a favor. Don't ever become a public speaker. You mumble, and your mannerisms are poor. There's no doubt you'll be a failure." Not long after that class, I made a decision to surrender my life to Jesus. That choice totally changed everything! I'd like to find that professor today and say, "Look what God can do."*

Maybe you've experienced other people saying the same kind of thing to you. Being called a failure can really hurt, and the words can affect you for a long time. God defines success and failure differently than the world does. That's why we have to be careful of whom we listen to. Most successful people are not afraid of failing. They would rather try and fail than not try at all. We have to be careful that we don't become so afraid of failure that we never achieve any of our goals.

To him who is able to keep you from stumbling and to present you before his glorious presence without fault and with great joy—to the only God our Savior be glory, majesty, power and authority, through Jesus Christ our Lord, before all ages, now and forevermore! Amen.

JUDE 1:24–25 NIV

Yet I am always with you; you [God] hold me by my right hand. You guide me with your counsel, and afterward you will take me into glory. Whom have I in heaven but you? And earth has nothing I desire besides you. My flesh and my heart may fail, but God is the strength of my heart and my portion forever.

PSALM 73:23–26 NIV

Not that I have already obtained all this, or have already arrived at my goal, but I press on to take hold of that for which Christ Jesus took hold of me. Brothers and sisters, I do not consider myself yet to have taken hold of it. But one thing I do: Forgetting what is behind and straining toward what is ahead, I press on toward the goal to win the prize for which God has called me heavenward in Christ Jesus.

PHILIPPIANS 3:12–14 NIV

Now that we know what we have—Jesus, this great High Priest with ready access to God—let's not let it slip through our fingers. We don't have a priest who is out of touch with our reality. He's been through weakness and testing, experienced it all—all but the sin. So let's walk right up to him and get what he is so ready to give. Take the mercy, accept the help.

HEBREWS 4:14–16 MSG

FAMILY

APP: *I come from a large Italian family. We had so much fun when I was growing up. Every holiday we got together at my grandparents' house. Being with all my cousins was amazing, and there was always plenty of food. I miss those times. Even though my grandparents have passed away, we still try to stay connected and get together when we can. Family has always been important to me.*

The family is essential to the development of people and nations. It's the very core of what makes up society. But there's a lot of confusion today about what makes up a family. In the past it was normally accepted that a family consisted of a husband, wife, and children. But this is no longer accepted as being a typical family unit.

The root of the problem is that the family is not an institution planned by humans. It was designed by God. The family is one of God's greatest resources. He created it, and we have been given the responsibility of keeping it going. But there's also another family that believers belong to: the family of God. This forever family is made up of believers who are connected through faith.

Let us not become weary in doing good, for at the proper time we will reap a harvest if we do not give up. Therefore, as we have opportunity, let us do good to all people, especially to those who belong to the family of believers.

GALATIANS 6:9–10 NIV

Anyone who does not provide for their relatives, and especially for their own household, has denied the faith and is worse than an unbeliever.

1 TIMOTHY 5:8 NIV

Wives, understand and support your husbands by submitting to them in ways that honor the Master. Husbands, go all out in love for your wives. Don't take advantage of them. Children, do what your parents tell you. This delights the Master no end. Parents, don't come down too hard on your children or you'll crush their spirits.

COLOSSIANS 3:18–21 MSG

These commandments that I give you today are to be on your hearts. Impress them on your children. Talk about them when you sit at home and when you walk along the road, when you lie down and when you get up.

DEUTERONOMY 6:6–7 NIV

Children are a gift from the LORD; they are a reward from him. Children born to a young man are like arrows in a warrior's hands. How joyful is the man whose quiver is full of them!

PSALM 127:3–5 NLT

FEAR

APP: *People can be afraid of almost anything.
There's agoraphobia—the fear of public places;
claustrophobia—the fear of closed-in spaces;
astraphobia—fear of thunder; hydrophobia—fear
of water; and pyrophobia—fear of fire. If you don't
suffer from any of these phobias, there are many
more to choose from. Some people are terrified of
failure, so they never attempt anything. Others are
afraid of what people think, so they withdraw into
the safety of their own little world. And just about
everybody at some point in their lives is afraid of
death and disease. Fear can consume us, causing us
to do crazy things, crippling us emotionally so we no
longer enjoy life the way God planned. But it doesn't
have to be this way.*

*God wants to deliver us from our fears and set us
free to enjoy life. To conquer fear we need to develop
a "God-consciousness" and recognize that no matter
where we are or what is happening, if we have a
personal relationship with God, Jesus is always with
us in every situation. We can always depend on Him
when we are afraid.*

God is our refuge and strength, an ever-present help in trouble. Therefore we will not fear, though the earth give way and the mountains fall into the heart of the sea, though its waters roar and foam and the mountains quake with their surging.

PSALM 46:1–3 NIV

There is no fear in love. But perfect love drives out fear, because fear has to do with punishment. The one who fears is not made perfect in love.

1 JOHN 4:18 NIV

"Peace I [Jesus] leave with you; my peace I give you. I do not give to you as the world gives. Do not let your hearts be troubled and do not be afraid."

JOHN 14: 27 NIV

"The LORD your God is with you, the Mighty Warrior who saves. He will take great delight in you; in his love he will no longer rebuke you, but will rejoice over you with singing."

ZEPHANIAH 3:17 NIV

**The Lord is with me; I will not be afraid.
What can mere mortals do to me?**
PSALM 118:6 NIV

I sought the LORD, and he answered me; he delivered me from all my fears. Those who look to him are radiant; their faces are never covered with shame.

PSALM 34:4–5 NIV

FORGIVENESS

APP: *A young man who murdered four people at a church and a missionary training center was depressed, lonely, and bitter. Matt was a disturbed guy searching for belonging. A guy who dabbled in the occult and raged online about the strict biblical curriculum his parents used to homeschool him. And even though he chose to continue to be homeschooled and his parents told him every day that he was loved, Matt felt rejected and marginalized, unable to forgive his tormentors. After killing four people, he shot himself. A few months after the shootings, Matt's family met the parents of two sisters whom their son had killed. The girls' parents forgave Matt and his parents.*

Forgiveness isn't easy to define; it's hard to grasp and is not easily done even in the best of circumstances. Forgiveness is about making a decision to move forward. It means we allow ourselves to be released from what has happened in the past. Holding grudges only causes bitterness to consume and paralyze us. We can't change the past, but we can change our response. It's hard to forgive and let go of the past unless we have experienced forgiveness. We can be forgiven—and forgive others—because of what Jesus did on the cross.

"If you forgive those who sin against you, your heavenly Father will forgive you. But if you refuse to forgive others, your Father will not forgive your sins."
MATTHEW 6:14–15 NLT

Then Peter came to him and asked, "Lord, how often should I forgive someone who sins against me? Seven times?" "No, not seven times," Jesus replied, "but seventy times seven!"
MATTHEW 18:21–22 NLT

I'll [God will] forever wipe the slate clean of their sins. Once sins are taken care of for good, there's no longer any need to offer sacrifices for them.
HEBREWS 10:17–18 MSG

Bear with each other and forgive one another if any of you has a grievance against someone. Forgive as the Lord forgave you.
COLOSSIANS 3:13 NIV

So we praise God for the glorious grace he has poured out on us who belong to his dear Son. He is so rich in kindness and grace that he purchased our freedom with the blood of his Son and forgave our sins. He has showered his kindness on us, along with all wisdom and understanding.
EPHESIANS 1:6–8 NLT

FREEDOM

APP: *There's a lot of buzz about freedom today—freedom from things like terrorism, stress, doubt, anxiety, and financial burdens. Gurus and counselors tell us that if we live a certain way, think the right thoughts, or even vote for a particular ideology, we can be free. Freedom is the power to act or speak or think without any restrictions forced on us from the outside. It may be a hard thing to wrap your mind around, but most of us would like to have the choice to do whatever we want. Imagine having the freedom to listen to music as loud as you want, or to have a bank account with an unlimited balance. Or how about being able to eat whatever and as much as you want? I can think of a huge list of things I'd like to do, but most of them only offer temporary freedom.*

Real freedom that we all crave isn't physical; it's spiritual. The best source of freedom is found in God's Son. Only Jesus can set us free. Every time I speak in a prison facility, I remind the inmates that they can be freer than people living on the outside, because true freedom is about the condition of one's heart.

It is for freedom that Christ has set us free. Stand firm, then, and do not let yourselves be burdened again by a yoke of slavery.

GALATIANS 5:1 NIV

When hard pressed, I cried to the LORD;
he brought me into a spacious place.
PSALM 118:5 NIV

Since the children are made of flesh and blood, it's logical that the Savior took on flesh and blood in order to rescue them by his death. By embracing death, taking it into himself, he destroyed the Devil's hold on death and freed all who cower through life, scared to death of death.

HEBREWS 2:14–15 MSG

Then Jesus turned to the Jews who had claimed to believe in him. "If you stick with this, living out what I tell you, you are my disciples for sure. Then you will experience for yourselves the truth, and the truth will free you." Surprised, they said, "But we're descendants of Abraham. We've never been slaves to anyone. How can you say, 'The truth will free you'?" Jesus said, "I tell you most solemnly that anyone who chooses a life of sin is trapped in a dead-end life and is, in fact, a slave. A slave is a transient, who can't come and go at will. The Son, though, has an established position, the run of the house. So if the Son sets you free, you are free through and through."

JOHN 8:31–36 MSG

FRIENDS

APP: *None of us was created to live as an isolated island. We all need a friend—someone special whom we can trust. We want someone who cares and is always there for us. A friend is someone whom we can tell everything to and they will not betray us. True friends stick by us in the good times and the bad. They always find time for us, even if they have to drop something else. Real friends give without wanting something back. These kinds of friends are hard to find. If we have a BF or a BFF, we are really fortunate. But to have friends, you also need to be one.*

There's nothing wrong with having a close group of friends. God designed us as social beings. But He's very much against the abuse and misuse of friendships. That's why it is important to examine friendship in light of the Bible and to look to Jesus as our example. He didn't play favorites or isolate Himself from those who didn't fit in. When our relationship with Jesus is right, it's easier to have healthy friendships.

A friend loves at all times, and is born, as is a brother, for adversity.

PROVERBS 17:17 AMPC

Oil and perfume rejoice the heart; so does the sweetness of a friend's counsel that comes from the heart.

PROVERBS 27:9 AMPC

Love must be sincere. Hate what is evil; cling to what is good. Be devoted to one another in love. Honor one another above yourselves.
ROMANS 12:9–10 NIV

Make no friendship with a man given to anger, nor go with a wrathful man, lest you learn his ways and entangle yourself in a snare.

PROVERBS 22:24–25 ESV

Two are better than one, because they have a good reward for their toil. For if they fall, one will lift up his fellow. But woe to him who is alone when he falls and has not another to lift him up!

ECCLESIASTES 4:9–10 ESV

A man of many companions may come to ruin, but there is a friend who sticks closer than a brother.

PROVERBS 18:24 ESV

FUTURE

APP: *There's a research group on the West Coast with nearly forty years of forecasting experience. Their core work is identifying emerging trends that will transform global society. Their objective is to create insights on trends for everything from health care to technology to human identity. People have always been intrigued by the future. Those who have had a steady diet of science fiction start to imagine what the future will be like. But no matter what claims are made, no one can accurately predict all that's going to happen in the future. The best forecasts are really just educated guesses.*

Changes in our society have not only increased in speed and intensity, but also in their unpredictability. How can anyone succeed when the future is so uncertain? It's not hard to see why so many people fear the future. One of the most important things we can do is include God in our plans. It's crazy to make plans without checking with God first. He's the only One who truly does know the future—and He's excited about guiding you through it. Talk with God for advice as you plan; then act on your plan as you trust Him.

"For I know the plans I have for you," declares the LORD, "plans to prosper you and not to harm you, plans to give you hope and a future. Then you will call on me and come and pray to me, and I will listen to you. You will seek me and find me when you seek me with all your heart."

JEREMIAH 29:11–13 NIV

Now listen, you who say, "Today or tomorrow we will go to this or that city, spend a year there, carry on business and make money." Why, you do not even know what will happen tomorrow. What is your life? You are a mist that appears for a little while and then vanishes. Instead, you ought to say, "If it is the Lord's will, we will live and do this or that." As it is, you boast in your arrogant schemes. All such boasting is evil.

JAMES 4:13–16 NIV

"Therefore I [Jesus] tell you, do not worry about your life, what you will eat or drink; or about your body, what you will wear. Is not life more than food, and the body more than clothes?"
MATTHEW 6:25 NIV

"But seek first his [God's] kingdom and his righteousness, and all these things will be given to you as well. Therefore do not worry about tomorrow, for tomorrow will worry about itself. Each day has enough trouble of its own."

MATTHEW 6:33–34 NIV

GAMBLING

APP: *My grandpa was a big man with a raspy voice who smoked big cigars. His business was gambling. One day my brother and I, along with our cousins, were pretending to gamble in the living room of my grandparents' house. We grabbed a deck of Grandpa's poker cards and were having a great time. Grandpa came in the room, scooped up the cards, and ripped them to shreds. "Don't you kids ever play with cards again. Gambling's not good for you," he said. We couldn't figure out why Grandpa got so upset—after all, we were only playing a game.*

Unfortunately, that's the attitude too many teens have about gambling. Lots of teens are placing bets on everything from professional basketball games to local high school sporting events, playing small poker games, and scratching off lottery tickets. Researchers say that teens with a gambling addiction are more likely to engage in unsafe sex, binge drinking, drug abuse, and skipping school. How does gambling affect our relationship with God? Even though the Bible doesn't use the word gambling, there are still some principles that apply to gambling. It really can shape how we view ourselves and others. And there's no doubt it affects our relationship with God.

A hard worker has plenty of food, but a person who chases fantasies ends up in poverty. The trustworthy person will get a rich reward, but a person who wants quick riches will get into trouble. Showing partiality is never good, yet some will do wrong for a mere piece of bread. Greedy people try to get rich quick but don't realize they're headed for poverty.

PROVERBS 28:19–22 NLT

Those who want to get rich fall into temptation and a trap and into many foolish and harmful desires that plunge people into ruin and destruction. For the love of money is a root of all kinds of evil. Some people, eager for money, have wandered from the faith and pierced themselves with many griefs.

1 TIMOTHY 6:9–10 NIV

Work willingly at whatever you do, as though you were working for the Lord rather than for people. Remember that the Lord will give you an inheritance as your reward, and that the Master you are serving is Christ.
COLOSSIANS 3:23–24 NLT

Just because something is technically legal doesn't mean that it's spiritually appropriate. If I went around doing whatever I thought I could get by with, I'd be a slave to my whims.

1 CORINTHIANS 6:12 MSG

GANGS

APP: *There's a huge gang problem in the United States. The city of Los Angeles now has the distinction of being the gang capital of the country. I used to think that the gang problem was limited to big cities like LA, Chicago, Miami, Detroit, and New York. But as I travel across the country, I've noticed that gangs are everywhere—even in small towns. Why? Two reasons: The first has to do with identity, while the second is about family. A lot of teens struggle with acceptance, security, and significance— three things that make up our identity. Gangs will accept anybody and give them security and significance. If you're a member of a gang, there's a common identity. Gangs also function like families, and this can be very appealing for teens who come from broken homes. But unfortunately, these "families" frequently engage in serious and violent behavior. We all want to feel like we have a place to belong. For too many teens, that place is a gang. God offers acceptance, security, and significance—without the conditions and baggage of a gang. But we can only receive our identity from Him if we surrender.*

Be a good citizen. All governments are under God. Insofar as there is peace and order, it's God's order. So live responsibly as a citizen. If you're irresponsible to the state, then you're irresponsible with God, and God will hold you responsible. Duly constituted authorities are only a threat if you're trying to get by with something. Decent citizens should have nothing to fear. Do you want to be on good terms with the government? Be a responsible citizen and you'll get on just fine, the government working to your advantage. But if you're breaking the rules right and left, watch out. The police aren't there just to be admired in their uniforms. God also has an interest in keeping order, and he uses them to do it. That's why you must live responsibly—not just to avoid punishment but also because it's the right way to live. That's also why you pay taxes—so that an orderly way of life can be maintained. Fulfill your obligations as a citizen. Pay your taxes, pay your bills, respect your leaders. Don't run up debts, except for the huge debt of love you owe each other. When you love others, you complete what the law has been after all along. The law code—don't sleep with another person's spouse, don't take someone's life, don't take what isn't yours, don't always be wanting what you don't have, and any other "don't" you can think of—finally adds up to this: Love other people as well as you do yourself. You can't go wrong when you love others. When you add up everything in the law code, the sum total is *love*. But make sure that you don't get so absorbed and exhausted in taking care of all your day-by-day obligations that you lose track of the time and doze off, oblivious to God. The night is about over, dawn is about to break. Be up and awake to what God is doing! God is putting the finishing touches on the salvation work he began when we first believed. We can't afford to waste a minute, must not squander these precious daylight hours in frivolity and indulgence, in sleeping around and dissipation, in bickering and grabbing everything in sight. Get out of bed and get dressed! Don't loiter and linger, waiting until the very last minute. Dress yourselves in Christ, and be up and about!

ROMANS 13:1–14 MSG

There is neither Jew nor Greek, there is neither slave nor free, there is no male and female, for you are all one in Christ Jesus.
GALATIANS 3:28 ESV

But Peter and the apostles answered, "We must obey God rather than men."

ACTS 5:29 ESV

GENOCIDE

APP: *The Holocaust is one of the worst moral crimes ever committed in human history. It's estimated that five to six million Jews in World War II were killed in this act of genocide. The word* genocide *did not exist before 1944. That's when a lawyer named Raphael Lemkin was looking for a way to describe the Nazi policies of systematic murder of European Jews. He created the word* genocide *by combining the Greek word* geno, *which means "race" or "tribe," and the Latin word* cide, *for "killing." It's difficult to comprehend how one group of people could commit such violent crimes with the intent of destroying the existence of another group.*

When the Holocaust ended more than sixty years ago, the world said, "Never again," yet crimes against humanity continue. Deliberate and systematic destruction in whole or part of ethnic, racial, religious, and national groups has occurred in places like Darfur, Bosnia, Rwanda, and the Sudan. Preventing genocide continues to be a global challenge to individuals and nations. How will you make a difference? In what ways can you organize others to help put a stop to this horrible crime?

Celebrate, nations, join the praise of his people. He avenges the deaths of his servants, pays back his enemies with vengeance, and cleanses his land for his people.

DEUTERONOMY 32:43 MSG

"Far be it from you to do such a thing—to kill the righteous with the wicked, treating the righteous and the wicked alike. Far be it from you! Will not the Judge of all the earth do right?"

GENESIS 18:25 NIV

What then shall we say? Is God unjust?
Not at all! For he says to Moses, "I will have
mercy on whom I have mercy, and I will have
compassion on whom I have compassion."
It does not, therefore, depend on human
desire or effort, but on God's mercy.
ROMANS 9:14–16 NIV

GOD—THE FATHER

APP: *God is three persons—the Father, the Son, and the Holy Spirit. Our relationship with Him is the most significant one in our lives. But there are many misconceptions about what God is really like. Some people think He's like a retired ball player who was great in His prime but spends most of His time sitting in a rocking chair on a porch in heaven. Others see Him as a motorcycle cop on a bike behind a cloud waiting for us to have fun, then He'll shut us down. Some people think God is like an urgent-care provider—you don't mess with Him unless you have a really big emergency! Still others think He's a cosmic vending machine: Do a good deed; He'll give you something in return.*

God the Father is so different from all of these. He is all-knowing, which means He knows absolutely everything: past, present, and future. God is present everywhere. There is no place you can go on this planet where He's not. It's part of His care for us. And God is all-powerful. There's nothing He cannot do. We have to decide how we are going to relate to God the Father. Will we ignore Him or totally trust and obey Him?

"The God who made the world and everything in it is the Lord of heaven and earth and does not live in temples built by human hands. And he is not served by human hands, as if he needed anything. Rather, he himself gives everyone life and breath and everything else. From one man he made all the nations, that they should inhabit the whole earth; and he marked out their appointed times in history and the boundaries of their lands. God did this so that they would seek him and perhaps reach out for him and find him, though he is not far from any one of us."

ACTS 17:24–27 NIV

Yet, you LORD, are our Father. We are the clay, you are the potter; we are all the work of your hand.

ISAIAH 64:8 NIV

Just think—you don't need a thing, you've got it all! All God's gifts are right in front of you as you wait expectantly for our Master Jesus to arrive on the scene for the Finale. And not only that, but God himself is right alongside to keep you steady and on track until things are all wrapped up by Jesus. God, who got you started in this spiritual adventure, shares with us the life of his Son and our Master Jesus. He will never give up on you. Never forget that.

1 CORINTHIANS 1:7–9 MSG

But when the time arrived that was set by God the Father, God sent his Son, born among us of a woman, born under the conditions of the law so that he might redeem those of us who have been kidnapped by the law. Thus we have been set free to experience our rightful heritage. You can tell for sure that you are now fully adopted as his own children because God sent the Spirit of his Son into our lives crying out, "Papa! Father!" Doesn't that privilege of intimate conversation with God make it plain that you are not a slave, but a child? And if you are a child, you're also an heir, with complete access to the inheritance.

GALATIANS 4:4–7 MSG

For all who are led by the Spirit of God are children of God. So you have not received a spirit that makes you fearful slaves. Instead, you received God's Spirit when he adopted you as his own children. Now we call him, "Abba, Father." For his Spirit joins with our spirit to affirm that we are God's children. And since we are his children, we are his heirs. In fact, together with Christ we are heirs of God's glory. But if we are to share his glory, we must also share his suffering.

ROMANS 8:14–17 NLT

GOLDEN RULE

APP: *Versions of the Golden Rule are stated in almost every ancient writing regarding behavioral instruction—including the New Testament, Talmud, Koran, and the Analects of Confucius. It's basically a moral rule that states everyone has a right to just treatment and a responsibility to ensure justice for others. If you behave in a certain way toward another but you are unwilling to be treated that way in the same situation, then you violate the rule. It is the most essential basis for the modern concept of human rights. It's a good standard to which different cultures can appeal in resolving conflict.*

The biblical version of the Golden Rule teaches us to behave toward others as we would like to have them behave toward us. We need to think more deeply about the effects our actions have on others as we interact with them, and in the process try to imagine ourselves on the receiving end of these deeds. Think about what a different world this would be if every single person lived by the Golden Rule. How would your own relationships be different if you practiced the Golden Rule more often?

"So in everything, do to others what you would have them do to you, for this sums up the Law and the Prophets."

MATTHEW 7:12 NIV

"You're familiar with the command to the ancients, 'Do not murder.' I'm [Jesus] telling you that anyone who is so much as angry with a brother or sister is guilty of murder. Carelessly call a brother 'idiot!' and you just might find yourself hauled into court. Thoughtlessly yell 'stupid!' at a sister and you are on the brink of hellfire. The simple moral fact is that words kill. This is how I want you to conduct yourself in these matters. If you enter your place of worship and, about to make an offering, you suddenly remember a grudge a friend has against you, abandon your offering, leave immediately, go to this friend and make things right. Then and only then, come back and work things out with God. Or say you're out on the street and an old enemy accosts you. Don't lose a minute. Make the first move; make things right with him. After all, if you leave the first move to him, knowing his track record, you're likely to end up in court, maybe even jail. If that happens, you won't get out without a stiff fine."

MATTHEW 5:21–26 MSG

Jesus replied: " 'Love the Lord your God with all your heart and with all your soul and with all your mind.' This is the first and greatest commandment. And the second is like it: 'Love your neighbor as yourself.' All the Law and the Prophets hang on these two commandments."

MATTHEW 22:37–40 NIV

GOSSIP

APP: *Gossip is one of the oldest and most common ways of sharing unconfirmed facts and viewpoints. It's not always bad, because there are a lot of newspapers that carry "gossip" columns that detail the social and personal lives of celebrities and the elite members of a community. But most of the time it refers to the spreading of dirt and misinformation. The ability to distribute these exaggerated facts can now happen at an astonishing speed through social networking sites like Facebook and Twitter. And there always seems to be an army of paparazzi waiting, moving around like ninjas to capture pictures of the personal lives of celebrities.*

Gossip churns out from deep inside our hearts and makes a disgusting mess wherever it lands. It can make us feel better temporarily, but it's an awful experience for whoever gets in the way! Distasteful language like gossip is tainted and ugly. Someone always gets hurt by it. The words that come out of our mouths have power to do damage or the potential for amazing good. Listen closely to the kind of talk coming from your mouth. If you don't like what you hear, ask God to put fresh words on your tongue.

A gossip betrays a confidence, but a trustworthy person keeps a secret.

PROVERBS 11:13 NIV

A perverse person stirs up conflict, and a gossip separates close friends.

PROVERBS 16:28 NIV

**The mouths of fools are their undoing,
and their lips are a snare to their very lives.
The words of a gossip are like choice morsels;
they go down to the inmost parts.**
PROVERBS 18:7–8 NIV

A gossip goes around telling secrets, so don't hang around with chatterers.

PROVERBS 20:19 NLT

"Don't pass on malicious gossip. Don't link up with a wicked person and give corrupt testimony. Don't go along with the crowd in doing evil and don't fudge your testimony in a case just to please the crowd."

EXODUS 23:1 MSG

Though some tongues just love the taste of gossip, those who follow Jesus have better uses for language than that. Don't talk dirty or silly. That kind of talk doesn't fit our style. Thanksgiving is our dialect.

EPHESIANS 5:4 MSG

GUILT

APP: *What do you do about guilty feelings? How much do you understand about guilt? The word* guilt *refers to a sense of wrongdoing—it's an emotional conflict that occurs from second thoughts about a specific action or thought. God's method for clearing away these feelings is through repentance—asking for forgiveness for our wrong actions and thoughts, and turning away from them. But sometimes we still are plagued with guilt. Why? It's because these guilty feelings have their source in something other than sin.*

Feelings of false guilt may come as a result of legalism imposed by others at church. Or they could be from painful childhood memories of abuse and feeling responsible for what happened. They could also come as a result of criticism from others who have set up false standards that you are supposed to measure up to. Don't let the devil or anyone else use feelings of false guilt to harass you. Keep short accounts with God about sin. Confess it and move on. If you still have guilty feelings, ask God to show you the source of this regret and to help you deal with it in a healthy way.

Then I acknowledged my sin to you and did not cover up my iniquity. I said, "I will confess my transgressions to the Lord." And you forgave the guilt of my sin.

PSALM 32:5 NIV

Oh, give me back my joy again; you have broken me—now let me rejoice. Don't keep looking at my sins. Remove the stain of my guilt. Create in me a clean heart, O God. Renew a loyal spirit within me.

PSALM 51: 8–10 NLT

Do not hold us guilty for the sins of our ancestors! Let your compassion quickly meet our needs, for we are on the brink of despair. Help us, O God of our salvation! Help us for the glory of your name. Save us and forgive our sins for the honor of your name.
PSALM 79:8–9 NLT

And since we have a great High Priest who rules over God's house, let us go right into the presence of God with sincere hearts fully trusting him. For our guilty consciences have been sprinkled with Christ's blood to make us clean, and our bodies have been washed with pure water. Let us hold tightly without wavering to the hope we affirm, for God can be trusted to keep his promise.

HEBREWS 10:21–23 NLT

HATE

APP: *There's way too much hatred in our world today. People have these intense feelings of dislike for animals, nonliving objects, other individuals, and entire people groups. These breed hate speeches and hate crimes. Some people even have hatred for themselves and their very existence. Why so much hate?*

I had the opportunity to hear a Hungarian Jew who survived the Holocaust speak to college students. She told of being humiliated by her captors and forced to go without water or toilet facilities for days. Ultimately, she lost most of her family members except for one sister before being freed. "It was all because of hatred for a religion," she told the audience. I was surprised that her words were not bitter. However, she quickly reminded students never to hate anyone. "You are the future," she said. "Let's make this world a better world. Don't ever hate. You can accomplish so much more with kind words. When you're told to hate someone, ask why?"

Imagine how different our world would be if people stopped hating others because of their race, ethnic background, or religion. But it all starts with loving God—only then can you learn to love others.

If someone says, "I love God," but hates a fellow believer, that person is a liar; for if we don't love people we can see, how can we love God, whom we cannot see?

1 John 4:20 NLT

"Do not hate a fellow Israelite in your heart. Rebuke your neighbor frankly so you will not share in their guilt."

Leviticus 19:17 NIV

Everyone who hates his brother is a murderer; and you know that no murderer has eternal life abiding in him.

1 John 3:15 NASB

Do not be surprised, my brothers and sisters, if the world hates you.

1 John 3:13 NIV

The wicked commit slow suicide; they waste their lives hating the good.

Psalm 34:21 MSG

"Everyone who does evil hates the light, and will not come into the light for fear that their deeds will be exposed."

John 3:20 NIV

If anyone claims, "I am living in the light," but hates a fellow believer, that person is still living in darkness.

1 John 2:9 NLT

HEAVEN

APP: *Every civilization in history has been shaped by the idea that we will live forever. The early Christians had a preoccupation with heaven. They were constantly thinking and talking about it. Part of the reason was because of the persecution they faced. They looked forward to living forever with Jesus. There's been a lot of talk and books published about near-death experiences. But we need to make sure we check out what's being said about heaven in God's Word to see if it's accurate.*

Heaven is a real place with real people where we will live with Jesus for the rest of time. There's an immediate heaven where Christians go when they die. Then there's the eternal one—the new earth and the new universe—where God will dwell with His people. The current death rate is 100 percent, but no one likes to talk about it. Jesus came to deliver us from death. If we don't know Him, we will fear death. Are you looking forward to going to heaven? Are you prepared? Don't forget to ask God to use you to help bring your family and friends along as well.

I lift up my eyes to you, to you who sit enthroned in heaven.

PSALM 123:1 NIV

"Look down from heaven, your holy dwelling place, and bless your people Israel and the land you have given us as you promised on oath to our ancestors, a land flowing with milk and honey."
DEUTERONOMY 26:15 NIV

The LORD is in his holy temple; the LORD is on his heavenly throne. He observes everyone on earth; his eyes examine them.

PSALM 11:4 NIV

In My Father's house there are many dwelling places (homes). If it were not so, I would have told you; for I am going away to prepare a place for you.

JOHN 14:2 AMPC

Surely your goodness and love will be with me all my life, and I will live in the house of the LORD forever.

PSALM 23:6 NCV

For we know that if the earthly tent we live in is destroyed, we have a building from God, an eternal house in heaven, not built by human hands.

2 CORINTHIANS 5:1 NIV

HELL

APP: *The bumper sticker on the small black car caught my attention. It was bright red with gold sparkle letters that read: "Hell—the hot place to be." This person definitely got part of the equation right. Hell is a very real place, and it's hot—but it's not a place you want to be. The Bible teaches that it's a site of eternal fire and punishment for those who reject God's offer of forgiveness for sin. Jesus warns against unbelief to keep us from experiencing agonizing, eternal punishment. It's hard to even imagine such a place as hell and why anyone would willingly want to go there. It was never God's plan to send anyone to hell. We make the choice to be separated from His love, forgiveness, and hope.*

It's important to choose wisely while we still can, because once we die, there are no second chances. Worldwide, three people die every second, 180 every minute, and nearly 11,000 every hour. If the Bible is correct about what happens after we die, then more than 250,000 people go to heaven or hell every day. What are you specifically doing to show your relatives, friends, and people you work with how to avoid hell and get to heaven?

"Then they will go away to eternal punishment, but the righteous to eternal life."

MATTHEW 25:46 NIV

"I [Jesus] am the Living One; I was dead, and now look, I am alive for ever and ever! And I hold the keys of death and Hades."

REVELATION 1:18 NIV

"Then He will also say to those on His left, 'Depart from Me, accursed ones, into the eternal fire which has been prepared for the devil and his angels.' "

MATTHEW 25:41 NASB

"This is how it will be at the end of the age. The angels will come and separate the wicked from the righteous and throw them into the blazing furnace, where there will be weeping and gnashing of teeth."

MATTHEW 13:49–50 NIV

"If your right eye causes you to stumble, gouge it out and throw it away. It is better for you to lose one part of your body than for your whole body to be thrown into hell."

MATTHEW 5:29 NIV

"You can enter God's Kingdom only through the narrow gate. The highway to hell is broad, and its gate is wide for the many who choose that way. But the gateway to life is very narrow and the road is difficult, and only a few ever find it."

MATTHEW 7:13–14 NLT

HELP

APP: *We can do two things with help. Get it or give it. We all do both. Who's your help line? It all depends on what you need. You can find help online for lots of things, including your Netbook, iPod, mobile phone, pets, and even a recipe for dessert. There's also a source where you can find answers to basic life questions. But what about when you need help with more gritty existence stuff, like how to handle the pain, fear of the future, loneliness, or finding purpose in life? Whom do you turn to? It's not easy to find someone who you can spill your guts to and know that what you told them won't show up on social media in the next few minutes. We want someone who will understand us, provide the answers we are looking for, and have the power to change our circumstances.*

When we need help, God should be the first place we go. If you take the time to explore His Word, you will find answers you need to any situation. The hard part is following His advice. Maybe things are pretty cool in your life right now, but are you looking around to see if a friend could use some help?

In my distress I called upon the Lord, and cried to my God for help; He heard my voice out of His temple, and my cry for help before Him came into His ears.

PSALM 18:6 NASB

Hear my cry for mercy as I call to you for help, as I lift up my hands toward your Most Holy Place.

PSALM 28:2 NIV

Our soul waits for the Lord; He is our help and our shield.

PSALM 33:20 NASB

But I cry to you for help, Lord; in the morning my prayer comes before you.

PSALM 88:13 NIV

Blessed are those whose help is the God of Jacob, whose hope is in the Lord their God.

PSALM 146:5 NIV

"In everything I did, I showed you that by this kind of hard work we must help the weak, remembering the words the Lord Jesus himself said: 'It is more blessed to give than to receive.' "
ACTS 20:35 NIV

HOLY SPIRIT

APP: *The Holy Spirit is God's spiritual presence in our lives. He's not a vague, ghostly shadow or impersonal force; He's a real person who was sent to live inside us when Jesus ascended into heaven. Everybody who has a relationship with God has the power of the Holy Spirit available to them. He makes us new creations and is an amazing source of power and hope. The Holy Spirit gives us power to live the Christian life and strength for extraordinary tasks. He helps us understand the Bible and how to worship God. The Holy Spirit helps us when we pray and is our guarantee that God will keep His promises to us. We need to rely on the Holy Spirit to produce love, joy, peace, patience, kindness, goodness, faithfulness, and self-control in our lives. He also tugs at our hearts and minds to convict us about our sinfulness so we realize how much we need God's love and forgiveness.*

If we really want to grow in our relationship with God, it's important that we don't do anything to hinder the Spirit's work in our lives. Can you think of a sinful habit that may be limiting His work in your life? Are you relying on the Holy Spirit's power to help you with problems you're struggling with?

As bad as you are, you still know how to give good gifts to your children. But your heavenly Father is even more ready to give the Holy Spirit to anyone who asks.

Luke 11:13 CEV

"But you will receive power when the Holy Spirit comes upon you. And you will be my witnesses, telling people about me everywhere—in Jerusalem, throughout Judea, in Samaria, and to the ends of the earth."

Acts 1:8 NLT

What we have received is not the spirit of the world, but the Spirit who is from God, so that we may understand what God has freely given us.

1 Corinthians 2:12 NIV

But the Holy Spirit produces this kind of fruit in our lives: love, joy, peace, patience, kindness, goodness, faithfulness.

Galatians 5:22 NLT

In the same way the Spirit also helps our weakness; for we do not know how to pray as we should, but the Spirit Himself intercedes for *us* with groanings too deep for words.

Romans 8:26 NASB

HONESTY

APP: *They could have cleaned the place completely out. But some honest shoppers at an unstaffed Dollar Tree store in Colorado decided that honesty still matters. About fifteen shoppers walked through the front doors of a closed Dollar Tree store on Labor Day after a door lock malfunctioned. Somehow they either didn't see the sign on the doors—or ignored it—saying the store was closed for the holiday on Monday. At first, nothing seemed out of place to the shoppers. The lights in the store were all on and music was playing in the background, making everything seem normal. But one shopper became suspicious when there was no one at the register to ring up her purchases and called the police. They were able to contact a manager who fixed the lock and closed the store. It's amazing that no one looted the store!*

There's an erosion of honesty in our society. It's awful when deceit is normal instead of shameful. It's hard to trust someone who's been dishonest; plus it ruins a lot of relationships. Are you honest with your friends? How about when a cashier gives you too much change? What about being honest with yourself about things you need to work on? Truth is always better than a lie.

"Do not steal. Do not lie. Do not deceive one another."

LEVITICUS 19:11 NIV

"Don't cheat when measuring length, weight, or quantity. Use honest scales and weights and measures. I am GOD, your God. I brought you out of Egypt."

LEVITICUS 19:35 MSG

An honest answer is like a kiss on the lips.

PROVERBS 24:26 NIV

The LORD hates dishonest scales, but he is pleased with honest weights.

PROVERBS 11:1 NCV

**Better to have little, with godliness,
than to be rich and dishonest.**
PROVERBS 16:8 NLT

But there will be rewards for those who live right and tell the truth, for those who refuse to take money by force or accept bribes, for all who hate murder and violent crimes.

ISAIAH 33:15 CEV

Also, do not wrong or cheat another Christian in this way. The Lord will punish people who do those things as we have already told you and warned you.

1 THESSALONIANS 4:6 NCV

HOPE

APP: It's pretty common today to feel down and bummed. It's no big surprise. Just look around. Families falling apart, the threat of terrorism, natural disasters, racism, a life that lacks purpose and more can make you feel pretty hopeless. The effects of hopelessness can be devastating. You get depressed and stressed. Boredom creeps in. It's tough to get motivated. People will do almost anything when they feel like there's no hope for the future. Some turn to drugs and alcohol to cope. For others, taking their own life might feel like the only option. So where do we find hope? . . . The kind of hope that lasts and will help us cope when life doesn't seem to be working. One place: Jesus. It's not just empty expectations and desires when you turn to Jesus for hope. When He's the source of your hope, you'll have confidence and motivation to hang in there. It's like an anchor that stabilizes your life. When Jesus died on the cross and came back to life after being in the grave three days, He proved He is the source of our hope. Life with Jesus is an endless hope. Life without Jesus is a hopeless end.

This hope is a strong and trustworthy anchor for our souls.

HEBREWS 6:19 NLT

GOD's loyal love couldn't have run out, his merciful love couldn't have dried up. They're created new every morning. How great your faithfulness!

LAMENTATIONS 3:23–24 MSG

I wait for the LORD, my whole being waits, and in his word I put my hope.

PSALM 130:5 NIV

"For I know the plans I have for you," declares the LORD, "plans to prosper you and not to harm you, plans to give you hope and a future."
JEREMIAH 29:11 NIV

For surely there is a hereafter, and your hope will not be cut off.

PROVERBS 23:18 NKJV

HYPOCRISY

APP: *Hypocrisy is a dangerous game of pretense. A hypocrite is a person who engages in a similar behavior he condemns in others. It's a form of deception that undermines trust in relationships. Have you noticed how easy it is to slip into hypocrisy? We can hammer friends or family members for the movies they watch, but we fail to see the same problem with Web sites we visit. Hypocrisy can show up in our language, habits, how we treat our parents, how we behave on dates, and what parties we attend. Nothing will undermine our ability to be an effective influence for Jesus more quickly than hypocrisy. We have to stop deceiving ourselves as to what we can get away with when we pretend to be something we're not in front of friends and family. They can spot a phony a mile away. People today are searching for role models who are real and genuine, individuals who live life with integrity and consistency. We have to remember to carefully examine our own lives first before judging or criticizing others. How far does your hypocrisy extend? In the struggle against hypocrisy, remember the issue is not perfection. But God does expect us to rely on His help and power to resist hypocrisy.*

You Pharisees and teachers are in for trouble! You're nothing but show-offs. You're like tombs that have been whitewashed. On the outside they are beautiful, but inside they are full of bones and filth. That's what you are like. Outside you look good, but inside you are evil and only pretend to be good.

MATTHEW 23:27–28 CEV

You can see the speck in your friend's eye, but you don't notice the log in your own eye. How can you say, "My friend, let me take the speck out of your eye," when you don't see the log in your own eye? You're nothing but show-offs! First, take the log out of your own eye. Then you can see how to take the speck out of your friend's eye.

MATTHEW 7:3–5 CEV

"And when you pray, do not be like the hypocrites, for they love to pray standing in the synagogues and on the street corners to be seen by others. Truly I tell you, they have received their reward in full. But when you pray, go into your room, close the door and pray to your Father, who is unseen. Then your Father, who sees what is done in secret, will reward you."

MATTHEW 6:5–6 NIV

IDENTITY

APP: *Who we are is not determined by what we do, by where we live or go to school, or even by the things we possess. There are a lot of misconceptions over what really makes up our true identity. A good way to clear up the confusion is to keep in mind that our identity is made up of security, acceptance, and significance. They're all things we want and need, but they're tough to find. We can end up doing some pretty crazy things to find our identity. And if we aren't successful finding it when we're young, we end up having an identity crisis as an adult. Being confused over our identity can make us frustrated and lack confidence, and we will not become the person God designed us to be. Knowing who you are is crucial to having a meaningful life. The only place you can find your real identity is in an intimate relationship with Jesus. We are secure in Him because He will never leave us. Jesus accepts us just the way we are and will never reject us. And what could be more significant than being a child of the living God? Have you grasped who you really are and all that God has designed you to be and experience?*

Anyone who belongs to Christ is a new person. The past is forgotten, and everything is new.

2 CORINTHIANS 5:17 CEV

For we are God's handiwork, created in Christ Jesus to do good works, which God prepared in advance for us to do.

EPHESIANS 2:10 NIV

See how very much our Father loves us, for he calls us his children, and that is what we are! But the people who belong to this world don't recognize that we are God's children because they don't know him.
1 JOHN 3:1 NLT

You Gentiles are no longer strangers and foreigners. You are citizens with everyone else who belongs to the family of God.

EPHESIANS 2:19 CEV

For if we are faithful to the end, trusting God just as firmly as when we first believed, we will share in all that belongs to Christ.

HEBREWS 3:14 NLT

Now you are the body of Christ, and each one of you is a part of it.

1 CORINTHIANS 12:27 NIV

IDOLS

APP: American Idol *seems light years away from a group of primitive people in a far-off land bowing down to stone idols. But there is a connection. Idols are people and things that we give excessive admiration, worship, or devotion to. They don't have to be primitive man-made objects you'd find on a remote island.*

Who or what are you worshipping? We make idols out of people like athletes, actors, singers—anyone who can influence another person. Sometimes we make idols out of friends, relationships, and even ourselves. We can also make idols out of normal everyday objects like our smart phones, iPads, or cars. Or for us it could be popularity, power, or money. All of these people and things are not necessarily bad unless they have captured our hearts in an unhealthy way.

The danger comes when we allow anyone or anything to come between us and God. It's good to have dreams of what we want to be and achieve, unless we leave God totally out of the picture. Who or what does your heart belong to? Have you allowed someone or something to come between you and your relationship with God? Check your life for idols that may need to be removed.

Children, you must stay away from idols.

1 JOHN 5:21 CEV

"You shall have no other gods before me."

EXODUS 20:3 NIV

Jesus said to him, "Away from me, Satan! For it is written: 'Worship the Lord your God, and serve him only.' "

MATTHEW 4:10 NIV

"I am the LORD; that is my name! I will not give my glory to anyone else, nor share my praise with carved idols."

ISAIAH 42:8 NLT

Everyone who worships idols as though they were gods will be terribly ashamed.

ISAIAH 42:17 CEV

**How foolish are those who manufacture idols.
These prized objects are really worthless.
The people who worship idols don't know
this, so they are all put to shame.**
ISAIAH 44:9 NLT

"Do not turn to idols or make metal gods for yourselves. I am the LORD your God."

LEVITICUS 19:4 NIV

IMMORTALITY

APP: *How long do you want to live? Some scientists claim it may be possible to live for 500 years in perfect health in the not-too-distant future. In biblical times people lived for long periods of time—much longer than we do today. Tales have been around for hundreds of years about a "fountain of youth." Legend has it that "eternal youth" belongs to anyone who drinks its water. What about life after death? Living forever in a physical or spiritual form is a hard concept to wrap your mind around. How can we even begin to imagine being alive for an inconceivably vast length of time? Questions flood our minds when we think about death not being the end. Ever since the beginning of human history, people have wondered what form unending life would take. But immortality shouldn't be a mystery for anyone who has a relationship with the living God. The resurrection of Jesus is our guarantee that we will live forever in heaven someday. It's God's gift to all those who would surrender their lives to Him. How does the assurance of immortality change the way you live your life each day?*

"For God so loved the world, that He gave His only begotten Son, that whoever believes in Him shall not perish, but have eternal life."

JOHN 3:16 NASB

"I tell you the truth, whoever hears what I say and believes in the One who sent me has eternal life. That person will not be judged guilty but has already left death and entered life."

JOHN 5:24 NCV

For the wages of sin is death, but the gift of God is eternal life in Christ Jesus our Lord.
ROMANS 6:23 NIV

You have made known to me the path of life; you will fill me with joy in your presence, with eternal pleasures at your right hand.

PSALM 16:11 NIV

"My sheep hear My voice, and I know them, and they follow Me; and I give eternal life to them, and they will never perish; and no one will snatch them out of My hand."

JOHN 10:27–28 NASB

And this is the testimony: God has given us eternal life, and this life is in his Son.

1 JOHN 5:11 NIV

INCEST

APP: *Any way you look at it, incest is ugly. The sexual abuse of a child by a relative or other person who's in a position of trust and authority is never right. It doesn't fly with what's culturally normal in most societies, and it's against the law (although in a few societies, it's practiced among royalty). Incest doesn't discriminate. It happens in all kinds of families. When it involves younger people, it's been proven to be one of the most extreme forms of childhood trauma. Lots of times there's intense pressure on the victim to keep silent because of the fear that the family may break up. Incest can have long-term effects on victims. They can end up struggling with everything from low self-esteem to depression to substance abuse. But we have an amazing God who loves us more than we will ever know and has the power to put broken lives back together again. You may not be a victim of incest, but chances are you know someone who is. Think about being part of God's long-term care in their life. Every incest victim needs the support of someone who cares about them and someone they can trust.*

"No one is to approach any close relative to have sexual relations. I am the Lord."

LEVITICUS 18:6 NIV

But among you there must not be even a hint of sexual immorality, or of any kind of impurity, or of greed, because these are improper for God's holy people.

EPHESIANS 5:3 NIV

"If a man marries his sister, the daughter of either his father or his mother, and they have sexual relations, it is a shameful disgrace. They must be publicly cut off from the community. Since the man has violated his sister, he will be punished for his sin."

LEVITICUS 20:17 NLT

"Cursed is anyone who sleeps with his sister, the daughter of his father or the daughter of his mother." Then all the people shall say, "Amen!"

DEUTERONOMY 27:22 NIV

It is God's will that you should be sanctified: that you should avoid sexual immorality.

1 THESSALONIANS 4:3 NIV

Don't be immoral in matters of sex. That is a sin against your own body in a way that no other sin is.

1 CORINTHIANS 6:18 CEV

INFLUENCE

APP: *Most everyone would admit they'd like to be a person of influence. Maybe that's why we are so consumed with celebrities and secretly wish for our fifteen minutes of fame. Who wouldn't want to have the power to affect, control, or manipulate something or someone? Imagine what it would be like to change the way people think, behave, or make decisions. How different would things be at home? How about at school? Where you work? Life in our part of the world could end up being totally different from what we're experiencing right now. But helpful influence is really more about persuasion than power. When Jesus said that we are "salt" and "light," He was talking about our influencing the quality of life of those around us in a positive way. But living in our society, it's easy to find ourselves being influenced by captivating leaders, friends, and even marketing. Think about the power of a sixty-second commercial to persuade us to buy, go, or do. You can choose to be influenced by people and things around you, or you can decide to be a person of influence. It's totally up to you.*

"In the same way, let your light shine before others, that they may see your good deeds and glorify your Father in heaven."

MATTHEW 5:16 NIV

Get the word out. Teach all these things. And don't let anyone put you down because you're young. Teach believers with your life: by word, by demeanor, by love, by faith, by integrity. Stay at your post reading Scripture, giving counsel, teaching. And that special gift of ministry you were given when the leaders of the church laid hands on you and prayed— keep that dusted off and in use.

1 TIMOTHY 4:11–14 MSG

So don't sit around on your hands! No more dragging your feet! Clear the path for long-distance runners so no one will trip and fall, so no one will step in a hole and sprain an ankle. Help each other out. And run for it!

HEBREWS 12:12–13 MSG

**When the LORD takes pleasure
in anyone's way, he causes their
enemies to make peace with them.**
PROVERBS 16:7 NIV

Cultivate these things. Immerse yourself in them. The people will all see you mature right before their eyes! Keep a firm grasp on both your character and your teaching. Don't be diverted. Just keep at it. Both you and those who hear you will experience salvation.

1 TIMOTHY 4:15–16 MSG

INTEGRITY

APP: *People of integrity live differently. There's a consistency in their lives that is based on a set of values that are important to them. They have a commitment to honesty and truthfulness that causes them to be authentic in the way they live instead of being a hypocrite. It's a quality that develops deep inside over time that enables them to know the right thing to do. But sadly there is an integrity crisis today. We live in a world that says there are no moral absolutes—no right or wrong. Compromise divides what happens in the government, at school, at home, and sometimes even in the church.*

How do you live and behave at home? What about school or work? Do you live consistently? What specific things do you need to change in your life to be a person of integrity? To be this kind of person means that you keep your word, live by what is right instead of what's convenient, and establish a biblical set of principles to live by. A person of integrity doesn't disagree with themselves and takes responsibility for their actions. What they say and how they live match.

The integrity of the upright guides them, but the unfaithful are destroyed by their duplicity.

PROVERBS 11:3 NIV

I know, my God, that you examine our hearts and rejoice when you find integrity there. You know I have done all this with good motives, and I have watched your people offer their gifts willingly and joyously.

1 CHRONICLES 29:17 NLT

Better the poor whose walk is blameless than the rich whose ways are perverse.

PROVERBS 28:6 NIV

People with integrity walk safely, but those who follow crooked paths will be exposed.

PROVERBS 10:9 NLT

Whoever tries to live right and be loyal finds life, success, and honor.
PROVERBS 21:21 NCV

May integrity and honesty protect me, for I put my hope in you.

PSALM 25:21 NLT

Because of my integrity you uphold me and set me in your presence forever.

PSALM 41:12 NIV

JEALOUSY

APP: *Have you taken the jealousy test? It supposedly helps you know what level of jealousy you are experiencing in a romantic relationship. Jealousy is a common experience in human relationships. It's so much a part of who we are that it can be seen even in the lives of babies less than a year old. Jealousy has been the theme of lots of poems, novels, songs, and films. Being "green-eyed" with jealousy can cause us to experience a combination of emotions, including anger and sadness, and it can even twist our stomachs into knots. Lots of times we use envy and jealousy as interchangeable words. But they're really very different. Jealousy is hoping to keep what you already have, while envy is hoping to get what you don't have. When we're jealous it has to do with identity, happiness, and comparing ourselves to others. Jealousy is a real-life problem that causes trouble in many relationships. It sets off bitterness, hurt, and anger. We have to learn to recognize it when it comes and deal with it in a healthy way. If we don't, we might end up struggling with feelings of inferiority and have trouble trusting others.*

A peaceful heart leads to a healthy body; jealousy is like cancer in the bones.

PROVERBS 14:30 NLT

You are jealous and argue with each other. This proves that you are not spiritual and that you are acting like the people of this world.

1 CORINTHIANS 3:3 CEV

Whenever people are jealous or selfish, they cause trouble and do all sorts of cruel things.
JAMES 3:16 CEV

Do not let your heart envy sinners, but always be zealous for the fear of the LORD.

PROVERBS 23:17 NIV

And I saw that all toil and all achievement spring from one person's envy of another. This too is meaningless, a chasing after the wind.

ECCLESIASTES 4:4 NIV

Let us not become conceited, provoking and envying each other.

GALATIANS 5:26 NIV

Anger is cruel, and wrath is like a flood, but jealousy is even more dangerous.

PROVERBS 27:4 NLT

JESUS CHRIST

APP: *Jesus is the most amazing person ever to live. There has never been anyone else like Him. Jesus never wrote a book or went to college. He never traveled more than 200 miles from His birthplace and lived only thirty-three years on earth. Yet Jesus lived the most influential life of anyone. More has been written about His life than any other figure in history. Jesus is the central figure of Christianity and has followers in every country of the world. He is totally unique. Jesus said and did things that no one else ever did. His physical body was 100 percent human, but He was also 100 percent God. By becoming a man, Jesus made it possible for us to relate to Him and for God to relate to us through Him. What's more, Jesus made it possible for us to experience unconditional love and forgiveness. He rose from the dead and gave convincing proof that He was alive. Jesus is the key for us to become part of God's family. Who is Jesus to you? What are you going to do with Him? This is the most important decision you will ever make.*

But God showed how much he loved us by having Christ die for us, even though we were sinful.

ROMANS 5:8 CEV

If you openly declare that Jesus is Lord and believe in your heart that God raised him from the dead, you will be saved.

ROMANS 10:9 NLT

At the name of Jesus every knee should bow, in heaven and on earth and under the earth, and every tongue declare that Jesus Christ is Lord, to the glory of God the Father.
PHILIPPIANS 2:10–11 NLT

But now you have been united with Christ Jesus. Once you were far away from God, but now you have been brought near to him through the blood of Christ.

EPHESIANS 2:13 NLT

And since we have been made right in God's sight by the blood of Christ, he will certainly save us from God's condemnation.

ROMANS 5:9 NLT

Jesus told him, "I am the way, the truth, and the life. No one can come to the Father except through me."

JOHN 14:6 NLT

JESUS IS GOD

APP: *Jesus was God's physical presence on earth. He is God and has always existed. There's a popular spiritual philosophy that says all religions lead to God and that Jesus was just a good teacher. That's nonsense. Jesus proved that He was God by doing tons of things that only God could do. He performed miracles, like when He made dead people alive again, walked across water, healed diseases with a word, or made blind people able to see again. How about when He created the universe and the planet we call home? Jesus claimed to be God and said He had the authority to forgive sins. He also accepted worship from His disciples. One of them named Thomas realized after Jesus' resurrection that He was God and humbly worshipped Him. Jesus made religious leaders angry when He said that He was the only way to God. Jesus declared His true identity many times, and it's very important that we understand this truth and grasp it. It's an amazing truth that will totally change the way we think and live. Do you really believe that Jesus is God? How has this affected your life?*

Jesus answered, "I tell you the truth, before Abraham was even born, I Am!"

JOHN 8:58 NLT

"Don't you believe that I am in the Father, and that the Father is in me? The words I say to you I do not speak on my own authority. Rather, it is the Father, living in me, who is doing his work."

JOHN 14:10 NIV

"All right then, the Lord himself will give you the sign. Look! The virgin will conceive a child! She will give birth to a son and will call him Immanuel (which means 'God is with us')."
ISAIAH 7:14 NLT

Jesus answered, "I tell you for certain that even before Abraham was, I was, and I am."

JOHN 8:58 CEV

The Son is the image of the invisible God, the firstborn over all creation. For in him all things were created: things in heaven and on earth, visible and invisible, whether thrones or powers or rulers or authorities; all things have been created through him and for him. He is before all things, and in him all things hold together.

COLOSSIANS 1:15–17 NIV

JUSTICE

APP: *Justice is concerned with the proper ordering of people and things within a society. It's a very important idea that has been debated throughout human history. What is justice, and what does it demand of individuals and societies? It is distinct from charity and compassion. Some define it as a view of moral rightness based on fairness and ethical values. But who decides what's fair and what should be the proper distribution of wealth and resources in society? Is the arrangement to be based on what is equal or status quo? It's a hotly debated subject that has often been associated with fate, reincarnation, or a cosmic plan for life. There are countless examples of injustice—acts that inflict undeserved hurt—in our world today. Many are crying out for justice in the midst of observing human suffering—whatever form it may be. Our God is a God of justice who will one day right the wrongs. We have to realize that life is not fair, but we also cannot simply ignore the injustice we see. As followers of Jesus, we must do all we can with God's help to seek justice for those who are not able to do so for themselves.*

The LORD loves righteousness and justice; the earth is full of his unfailing love.

PSALM 33:5 NIV

"Give justice to the poor and the orphan; uphold the rights of the oppressed and the destitute."

PSALM 82:3 NLT

Vindicate the weak and fatherless; do justice to the afflicted and destitute.

PSALM 82:3 NASB

The LORD God has told us what is right and what he demands: "See that justice is done, let mercy be your first concern, and humbly obey your God."
MICAH 6:8 CEV

Your kingdom is ruled by justice and fairness with love and faithfulness leading the way.

PSALM 89:14 CEV

If a king judges the poor with fairness, his throne will be established forever.

PROVERBS 29:14 NIV

LIE / LYING

APP: *Lying ruins relationships. Planning to deceive others with statements that aren't true, trying to avoid punishment for your actions, or denying others access to information they are entitled to isn't a healthy thing to do. Think about friends or family members who lie to you. How do you feel about them? It's tough to trust someone who sets out to deceive you, because then you never know when they're telling the truth or when they're lying. There's a difference between bluffing and lying. Bluffing usually takes place in a game where players agree in advance that it's okay. For example, athletes "fake it" in games all the time. A ball player hints that he will move to the left then dodges to the right. Exaggerating is also different from lying, but it still can easily get out of control. By "stretching the truth," we make something more powerful or meaningful than it really is. Lying has become a big problem, because there are no moral absolutes in our culture. People no longer agree on rules that manage behavior, but this still doesn't make it okay to practice deceiving others.*

Truthful lips endure forever, but a lying tongue lasts only a moment.

PROVERBS 12:19 NIV

Do not steal or tell lies or cheat others.

LEVITICUS 19:11 CEV

The LORD detests lying lips, but he delights in those who tell the truth.

PROVERBS 12:22 NLT

Telling lies about others is as harmful as hitting them with an ax, wounding them with a sword, or shooting them with a sharp arrow.
PROVERBS 25:18 NLT

The crooked heart will not prosper; the lying tongue tumbles into trouble.

PROVERBS 17:20 NLT

Does anyone want to live a life that is long and prosperous? Then keep your tongue from speaking evil and your lips from telling lies!

PSALM 34:12–13 NLT

LONELINESS

APP: *Everyone experiences loneliness. Feeling empty, unwanted, or unimportant isn't unusual or something that's new to this generation. Some researchers suggest that it could have started way back during prehistoric times. Hunter-gatherers may have deliberately stayed away from others so they wouldn't have to share food they had collected. Loneliness is not the same as being alone. Loneliness is unwanted isolation that can even be experienced in crowded places. But being alone is a choice that can be a positive experience that emotionally recharges you if you are in control of the situation. Craving love or companionship can lead to some pretty strong emotions, such as rejection, depression, insecurity, resentment, and hopelessness. That's why it's good for us to learn how to cope with loneliness.*

When we have a personal relationship with God, we are never alone, because God's Spirit lives inside us. But we don't always feel His presence. One thing that can help is to hang out with others or get involved in activities where we can meet people. Another way to cope with loneliness is to look around and reach out to others who might also be lonely.

The Lord has promised that he will not leave us or desert us.

HEBREWS 13:5 CEV

I [Jesus] won't leave you like orphans. I will come back to you.

JOHN 14:18 CEV

And I will be your Father, and you will be my sons and daughters, says the LORD Almighty."

2 CORINTHIANS 6:18 NLT

Wherever you go, I will watch over you, then later I will bring you back to this land. I won't leave you—I will do all I have promised.
GENESIS 28:15 CEV

Answer me when I call to you, my righteous God. Give me relief from my distress; have mercy on me and hear my prayer.

PSALM 4:1 NIV

But let all who take refuge in you be glad; let them ever sing for joy. Spread your protection over them, that those who love your name may rejoice in you.

PSALM 5:11 NIV

LOVE

APP: Love truly is the greatest gift, but most people search for it in all the wrong places. In fact, culture has gotten so far away from true love and its meaning that most people don't even know what they're looking for.

Over and over again we've experience disappointment with love. For some, we've watched our parents' love fail, resulting in divorce. For others, you've been in a relationship where someone says "I love you," but then they left you in the dust for another. Maybe you've experienced love that is conditional—based on "I'll love you if you do this for me."

If you're tired of being let down and don't feel like getting your heart stomped on anymore, maybe it's time you went to the source of unfailing love— God Himself. He is love, and His love will never let you down. His promise of love appears lots of times in the Bible. (It's one of many promises you can depend on.) Nothing you could ever do or say will make God stop loving you. His love is unconditional and will last forever. God proved His love when Jesus died on the cross in our place. There's no greater love we could ever experience. Don't ever forget that God's crazy about you.

Love is patient and kind. Love is not jealous or boastful or proud or rude. It does not demand its own way. It is not irritable, and it keeps no record of being wronged. It does not rejoice about injustice but rejoices whenever the truth wins out. Love never gives up, never loses faith, is always hopeful, and endures through every circumstance.

1 CORINTHIANS 13:4–7 NLT

For God so loved the world that He gave His only begotten Son, that whoever believes in Him should not perish but have everlasting life.

JOHN 3:16 NKJV

But God showed his great love for us by sending Christ to die for us while we were still sinners.

ROMANS 5:8 NLT

And I am convinced that nothing can ever separate us from God's love. Neither death nor life, neither angels nor demons, neither our fears for today nor our worries about tomorrow—not even the powers of hell can separate us from God's love. No power in the sky above or in the earth below—indeed, nothing in all creation will ever be able to separate us from the love of God that is revealed in Christ Jesus our Lord.

ROMANS 8:38–39 NLT

**He who does not love does not
know God, for God is love.**
1 JOHN 4:8 NKJV

LUST

APP: *Lust is a struggle for lots of people living in our seductive culture. Being bombarded daily with advertising for material stuff can cause us to have an uncontrolled appetite for bling and bank. These intense feelings or cravings for things like cars, clothes, and cash can easily own our emotions and consume us. But even worse can be intense feelings of sexual desire. These thoughts and feelings can quickly and easily become uncontrolled in our life. And it's not just a guy thing. Girls struggle with lust just like guys do. And all of us can have trouble sorting through our emotions to discover if we are dealing with lust or love. We might think that we really care about someone when instead we really are craving them.*

Lust can get so intense and out of control that we end up in a type of emotional prison. It can be a tough one to escape from. But if we truly want to escape from the bondage of lust, God can give us the strength and courage we need to be free. It takes time and discipline, but with His help it's doable.

Behave like obedient children. Don't let your lives be controlled by your desires, as they used to be.

1 PETER 1:14 CEV

Don't lust for her beauty. Don't let her coy glances seduce you.

PROVERBS 6:25 NLT

"But I tell you that if anyone looks at a woman and wants to sin sexually with her, in his mind he has already done that sin with the woman."

MATTHEW 5:28 NCV

And because we belong to Christ Jesus, we have killed our selfish feelings and desires.

GALATIANS 5:24 CEV

Dear friends, I warn you as "temporary residents and foreigners" to keep away from worldly desires that wage war against your very souls.

1 PETER 2:11 NLT

Instead, clothe yourself with the presence of the Lord Jesus Christ. And don't let yourself think about ways to indulge your evil desires.

ROMANS 13:14 NLT

For everything in the world—the lust of the flesh, the lust of the eyes, and the pride of life—comes not from the Father but from the world.

1 JOHN 2:16 NIV

MARRIAGE

APP: *People marry for lots of reasons—including legal, economical, social, emotional, and spiritual. In some cultures, marriages are still being arranged today. But marriage is not doing well in our society between the confusion over how to define it and the high divorce rate. The problem has come about over time as we have gradually forgotten who designed the institution of marriage and for what purpose. Humans did not bring about marriage; God did way back in human history. According to the Bible, God's plan for marriage between a man and a woman is the very foundation for societies and nations. It's popular in our culture for people to say that marriage is just a piece of paper. Not according to God. This bond is so strong in His eyes that it is to only be broken by death. Marriage is never easy. The pressure on this institution of God's is enormous in our culture today. A husband and wife have to be totally committed to God and one another, working hard together for it to survive. If there's unconditional love and a willingness to forgive, with God's help marriage can be an awesome experience.*

Give honor to marriage, and remain faithful to one another in marriage. God will surely judge people who are immoral and those who commit adultery.

HEBREWS 13:4 NLT

"Haven't you read the Scriptures?" Jesus replied. "They record that from the beginning 'God made them male and female.'" And he said, "'This explains why a man leaves his father and mother and is joined to his wife, and the two are united into one.' Since they are no longer two but one, let no one split apart what God has joined together."

MATTHEW 19:4–6 NLT

Don't team up with those who are unbelievers. How can righteousness be a partner with wickedness? How long can light live with darkness?

2 CORINTHIANS 6:14 NLT

A truly good wife is the most precious treasure a man can find! Her husband depends on her, and she never lets him down. She is good to him every day of her life.

PROVERBS 31:10–12 CEV

In the same way, you husbands must give honor to your wives. Treat your wife with understanding as you live together. She may be weaker than you are, but she is your equal partner in God's gift of new life. Treat her as you should so your prayers will not be hindered.

1 PETER 3:7 NLT

MIND

APP: *How many handheld electronic devices do you own? Maybe you have a smart phone that enables you to do a variety of tasks—everything from texting to searching the Internet to listening to your favorite tunes. As high-tech as your device may be, it has nowhere near the capabilities that your mind has. Imagine being able to record, store, and categorize millions of bits of information in seconds. This happens in spite of experiencing feelings of brain overload at school. And even though we have a "brain freeze" from time to time, our minds can process amazingly complex things. There will never be a computer that can come close to the capacity for unlimited apps like our mind. But we need to be careful what we allow into our minds through our eyes and ears. What we think about is what we will become. We read, watch, or listen to something, and it floats around in our brain. These things shape our thoughts. Our thoughts shape our attitudes. Then our attitudes influence the way we live. Be deliberate in monitoring your thinking and the music you listen to; the TV shows you watch and where you go online. The more you read and apply the Bible, the easier it will be.*

And the peace of God, which transcends all under-standing, will guard your hearts and your minds in Christ Jesus.

PHILIPPIANS 4:7 NIV

Be alert and think straight. Put all your hope in how kind God will be to you when Jesus Christ appears.

1 PETER 1:13 CEV

Finally, my friends, keep your minds on whatever is true, pure, right, holy, friendly, and proper. Don't ever stop thinking about what is truly worthwhile and worthy of praise.

PHILIPPIANS 4:8 CEV

Those who live according to the flesh have their minds set on what the flesh desires; but those who live in accordance with the Spirit have their minds set on what the Spirit desires.

ROMANS 8:5 NIV

I appeal to you, brothers and sisters, in the name of our Lord Jesus Christ, that all of you agree with one another in what you say and that there be no divisions among you, but that you may be perfectly united in mind and thought.

1 CORINTHIANS 1:10 NIV

You must have the same attitude that Christ Jesus had.
PHILIPPIANS 2:5 NLT

MIRACLES

APP: *An incident that happens and is not fully explainable by the "known laws of nature" is a miracle. Some might say it's a result of a mystical force. Based on what the Bible teaches, we know that a miracle is an act of a loving God. Miracles are signs of God demonstrating His power and character in amazing ways. Sometimes there's a question about how to accept what happened. Do we believe it as a fact, or do we doubt? Just because we can't explain miracles doesn't mean they don't really happen. God can work any way He chooses—through created nature or by divine intervention. He can do absolutely anything He wants to; He's God.*

Think about all the miracles Jesus performed during His ministry on earth. He healed people, cast out demons, restored a severed ear, and raised the dead. Jesus even exercised control over nature by calming the sea and walking on water. People today think it's unscientific to believe in miracles. But not when you know the living God. He's still in the business of performing miracles. And don't miss what seem to be little day-to-day miracles like waking up in the morning—lots of people slip into eternity each night.

This miraculous sign at Cana in Galilee was the first time Jesus revealed his glory. And his disciples believed in him.

JOHN 2:11 NLT

In Jerusalem during Passover many people put their faith in Jesus, because they saw him work miracles.

JOHN 2:23 CEV

He gives one person the power to perform miracles, and another the ability to prophesy. He gives someone else the ability to discern whether a message is from the Spirit of God or from another spirit. Still another person is given the ability to speak in unknown languages, while another is given the ability to interpret what is being said.

1 CORINTHIANS 12:10 NLT

First, God chose some people to be apostles and prophets and teachers for the church. But he also chose some to work miracles or heal the sick or help others or be leaders or speak different kinds of languages.

1 CORINTHIANS 12:28 CEV

In Egypt and at the Red Sea and in the desert, Moses rescued the people by working miracles and wonders for forty years.

ACTS 7:36 CEV

MONEY

APP: *Money—we need it to get bling as well as the basic necessities of life. We can't live without money, and we usually find ourselves in a position of needing more of it. Whether it's plastic or cash, it's accepted as payment for goods and services along with repayment of debts. Jesus spoke more about money than any other topic—including heaven and hell—except the kingdom of God. Jesus knew that there is a major connection between our spiritual life and our attitudes and actions concerning money and possessions. He recognized the potential danger for being consumed by the pursuit of acquiring money and basing our security on it instead of faith in God. But there's also the potential for generosity. He didn't condemn possessions or commend poverty. But he does want us to "get" how important money is and how to properly use it. Part of having the right "money 'tude" is understanding that it all comes from God and we are supposed to wisely use how much He gives us. This is especially true for those of us living in North America, because we are some of the wealthiest people in the world.*

You cannot be the slave of two masters! You will like one more than the other or be more loyal to one than the other. You cannot serve both God and money.

MATTHEW 6:24 CEV

Wealth from get-rich-quick schemes quickly disappears; wealth from hard work grows over time.
PROVERBS 13:11 NLT

My God will use his wonderful riches in Christ Jesus to give you everything you need.

PHILIPPIANS 4:19 NCV

"Keep your life free from love of money, and be content with what you have."

HEBREWS 13:5 RSV

It is better to be godly and have little than to be evil and rich.

PSALM 37:16 NLT

All the Lord's followers often met together, and they shared everything they had. They would sell their property and possessions and give the money to whoever needed it.

ACTS 2:44–45 CEV

MURDER

APP: *Killing another person with intent is a senseless act. Murder deprives the victim of their right to exist. Most societies—past and present—consider murder the most serious crime you can commit. It's a crime that is worthy of the harshest punishment known to humanity. Bloodshed and violence are occasionally mentioned in the record of human history found in the Bible, but never with approval, except specific situations, as when the Israelites were to exterminate the Amalekites in obedience to God's command. Though in every situation it was because these offenders had become so wicked that had they lived, it would have resulted in spreading evil among the people committed to God. News outlets remind us daily how this senseless act continues to increase at an alarming rate. It's because we don't value human life and see it as precious anymore.*

A sixteen-year-old gang member arrested for murder was asked why he committed the crime. "I wanted to see what it felt like to kill someone," he responded. Life is sacred to God. Because He created life, He's the only One who has the right to take it. But remember you don't need to shoot someone to have murder in your heart. All you have to do is to hate them.

Jesus replied, " 'You shall not murder, you shall not commit adultery, you shall not steal, you shall not give false testimony, honor your father and mother,' and 'love your neighbor as yourself.' "

MATTHEW 19:18–19 NIV

"Whoever sheds human blood, by humans let his blood be shed, because God made humans in his image reflecting God's very nature. You're here to bear fruit, reproduce, lavish life on the Earth, live bountifully!"
GENESIS 9:6–7 MSG

Everyone who hates a brother or sister is a murderer, and you know that no murderers have eternal life in them.

1 JOHN 3:15 NCV

For let none of you suffer as a murderer, or a thief, or an evil-doer, or as a meddler in other men's matters.

1 PETER 4:15 ASV

MUSIC

APP: *Music is one of the most powerful and underestimated influences in our lives. It has the capacity to change our attitudes, beliefs, values, opinions, relationships, and even lifestyle choices. It can become a dangerous blind spot when we don't recognize how powerful it can be in our lives. We live in a music-saturated culture and closely identify with it. Music helps us to express our feelings, problems, pleasure, and beliefs. It reflects and directs our culture. For a lot of people, music produces lifestyles to adopt and cultural heroes to look up to and imitate. Artists and bands often set the pace for the way we dress, what we think, and what we do. But when you think about the ability music has to influence us, it's really not the style that we need to be concerned about. Musicians and songwriters use lyrics to communicate a message about how they think we should live. We have to carefully examine the philosophies songs are encouraging through the lyrics. We can find negative messages and deceptive philosophies no matter what style we listen to. That's why we have to learn to evaluate music based on the timeless principles of God's Word.*

Come, let us sing for joy to the Lord; let us shout aloud to the Rock of our salvation. Let us come before him with thanksgiving and extol him with music and song. For the Lord is the great God, the great King above all gods.

PSALM 95:1–3 NIV

Let them praise his name with dancing and make music to him with timbrel and harp.

PSALM 149:3 NIV

"Sing to the Lord, all the earth; proclaim his salvation day after day. Declare his glory among the nations, his marvelous deeds among all peoples."
1 CHRONICLES 16:23–24 NIV

I will sing to the Lord because he is good to me.

PSALM 13:6 NLT

Oh, sing to the Lord a new song! For He has done marvelous things; His right hand and His holy arm have gained Him the victory.

PSALM 98:1 NKJV

Make a joyful noise to the Lord, all you lands! Serve the Lord with gladness! Come before His presence with singing!

PSALM 100:1–2 AMPC

OBESITY

APP: *Obesity is a serious health issue affecting a lot of people today. It's the leading preventable cause of death worldwide and one of the most serious health problems of the twenty-first century. It's strange to think that at other times in history obesity was thought of as a symbol of wealth and fertility and still is in many parts of Africa today. With most people obesity is caused by eating too much and not getting enough exercise. The bad news is that obesity increases the possibility of having heart problems and difficulty breathing while you sleep; and getting a disease like type 2 diabetes or certain kinds of cancer. The treatment for it is simple—dieting and exercise—but it's not an easy thing to do if you're struggling with it. The cool thing is that we have a God who not only cares about our health, He can also give us the power to change our physical condition. Obesity may not be something you struggle with, but chances are you have a friend or family member who does. Look for ways to be an encouragement and a help to them.*

Do not be with heavy drinkers of wine, *or* with gluttonous eaters of meat; for the heavy drinker and the glutton will come to poverty, and drowsiness will clothe *one* with rags.

PROVERBS 23:20–21 NASB

It's not good to eat too much honey, and it's not good to seek honors for yourself.
PROVERBS 25:27 NLT

Don't go and stuff yourself! That would be just the same as cutting your throat.

PROVERBS 23:2 CEV

Then God said, "I give you every seed-bearing plant on the face of the whole earth and every tree that has fruit with seed in it. They will be yours for food."

GENESIS 1:29 NIV

A person without self-control is like a city with broken-down walls.

PROVERBS 25:28 NLT

Don't copy the behavior and customs of this world, but let God transform you into a new person by changing the way you think. Then you will learn to know God's will for you, which is good and pleasing and perfect.

ROMANS 12:2 NLT

THE OCCULT

APP: *There are many definitions of the occult and not much agreement on what it is. Many people would say that it's a mysterious practice that involves the influence of supernatural activity and secret knowledge. It goes beyond our natural senses to manipulate our—or someone else's—present or future lives. Because of the lack of agreement, some people would separate it into three main categories: divination, magic, and religious and spiritual quests. Divination includes various techniques of predicting the future, such as astrology, I Ching, numerology, palm reading, runes, scrying, and tarot cards. Magick is about practicing different kinds of spells and rituals. These are supposed to be able to change the material world and the environment to reach the goals of the person practicing them. Religious and spiritual quests usually involve a combination of alternative religions like vodun, Santeria, satanism, Wicca, Hinduism, Buddhism, and Taoism. These things may seem fascinating, but they are evil in God's eyes. A lot of our curiosity with these things might be coming from a desire to want to know and control the future. But God wants us to trust Him with our todays and tomorrows.*

And when you look up to the sky and see the sun, the moon and the stars—all the heavenly array—do not be enticed into bowing down to them and worshiping things the Lord your God has apportioned to all the nations under heaven.

DEUTERONOMY 4:19 NIV

"Do not turn to mediums or seek out spiritists, for you will be defiled by them. I am the Lord your God."
LEVITICUS 19:31 NIV

"I will resolutely reject persons who dabble in the occult or traffic with mediums, prostituting themselves in their practices. I will cut them off from their people. Set yourselves apart for a holy life. *Live* a holy life, because I am God, your God. Do what I tell you; *live* the way I tell you. I am the God who makes you holy."

LEVITICUS 20:6–8 MSG

Someone may say to you, "Let's ask the mediums and those who consult the spirits of the dead. With their whisperings and mutterings, they will tell us what to do." But shouldn't people ask God for guidance? Should the living seek guidance from the dead? Look to God's instructions and teachings! People who contradict his word are completely in the dark.

ISAIAH 8:19–20 NLT

PAIN

APP: *I've lost track of the number of times I've been asked by students, "How do you handle the pain?" Sometimes life sucks. It's no wonder with all the abuse, suicide, divorce, rejection, loneliness, violence, and disease all around us. What do you do when you feel like you don't want to live anymore? Who do you turn to for help? God has answers, and He wants to relieve the pain and walk with us through the tough times. It's never easy, but we can make it through the most difficult times if we focus on Him instead of our circumstances. We will never be able to find an explanation for all the situations in life. God wants us to realize that He's in control no matter what is happening. It also helps to understand that suffering is a natural part of life. Jesus promised that we would experience pain and that He has a purpose for allowing it in our lives. When pain and suffering strike, we have to put our confidence in God and not give up. The more we really get to know Him through prayer and studying the Bible, the better we will be able to make it through the storms of life.*

Beloved, do not think it strange concerning the fiery trial which is to try you, as though some strange thing happened to you; but rejoice to the extent that you partake of Christ's sufferings, that when His glory is revealed, you may also be glad with exceeding joy. If you are reproached for the name of Christ, blessed *are you,* for the Spirit of glory and of God rests upon you. On their part He is blasphemed, but on your part He is glorified.

1 Peter 4:12–14 NKJV

And the God of all grace, who called you to his eternal glory in Christ, after you have suffered a little while, will himself restore you and make you strong, firm and steadfast.
1 Peter 5:10 NIV

Brothers and sisters, as an example of patience in the face of suffering, take the prophets who spoke in the name of the Lord. As you know, we count as blessed those who have persevered. You have heard of Job's perseverance and have seen what the Lord finally brought about. The Lord is full of compassion and mercy.

James 5:10–11 NIV

"Don't be afraid, for I am with you. Don't be discouraged, for I am your God. I will strengthen you and help you. I will hold you up with my victorious right hand."

Isaiah 41:10 NLT

PARENTS

APP: *Most of us have experienced times when we'd give anything to trade our parents in for new ones or send them on a space shuttle to a place no human has ever gone before. Some of us get this urge almost every day. At the very least we wish our parents would buy decent groceries for once, send our younger sister to a foreign country permanently, or buy us the car of our dreams. But sometimes the concerns we have with our parents are much more serious. We wish they would stop fighting, understand us, get back together again, or love us. Our relationship with Mom and Dad can often be awkward and tough. Things get even more complicated if you live with just one parent or a stepparent. If we're going to survive at home, we have to realize that God gave us parents as part of His protective plan to guide us and help us develop into the people He designed us to be. As you check out what God has to say in His Word about getting along with your parents, take it seriously. You might be surprised how this relationship might improve.*

Children, obey your parents in the Lord, for this is right. "Honor your father and mother"—which is the first commandment with a promise—"so that it may go well with you and that you may enjoy long life on the earth."

 EPHESIANS 6:1–3 NIV

"Honor your father and your mother,
so that you may live long in the land
the LORD your God is giving you."
EXODUS 20:12 NIV

Listen, my son, to your father's instruction and do not forsake your mother's teaching. They are a garland to grace your head and a chain to adorn your neck.

PROVERBS 1:8–9 NIV

Listen to your father, who gave you life, and do not despise your mother when she is old.

PROVERBS 23:22 NIV

Children's children are a crown to the aged, and parents are the pride of their children.

PROVERBS 17:6 NIV

PAST

APP: *The past is ancient history. It's completed and finished. The past is time that has elapsed in your life that you can never get back again. You can't change the past, but you can learn from it. Some people allow the past to define them. They want to use past experience to justify the way they are living in the present. Sometimes it becomes a sort of game where they become the victim and they blame others for the way they are today. When we make that choice, it affects our friendships and relationships in negative ways. It also limits the potential of what we can accomplish. Other people run from their past. They have things to keep secret from an earlier time in their life that they don't want anyone else to know about or deal with. Either way we lose. If we really want to live the way that God designed us to, we need to walk ahead of the past. It means we understand that we can only change our today and tomorrow; however, the past can provide us with valuable lessons and reminders. The only way the past will define us is if we choose to allow it to happen.*

Therefore, if anyone is in Christ, the new creation has come: The old has gone, the new is here!

2 CORINTHIANS 5:17 NIV

He [God] has removed our sins as far from us as the east is from the west.

PSALM 103:12 NLT

If we confess our sins, He is faithful and righteous to forgive us our sins and to cleanse us from all unrighteousness.

1 JOHN 1:9 NASB

He brought me up out of the pit of destruction, out of the miry clay, and He set my feet upon a rock making my footsteps firm. He put a new song in my mouth, a song of praise to our God; many will see and fear and will trust in the LORD.
PSALM 40:2–3 NASB

Look to the LORD and his strength; seek his face always. Remember the wonders he has done, his miracles, and the judgments he pronounced, you his servants, the descendants of Israel, his chosen ones, the children of Jacob.

1 CHRONICLES 16:11–13 NIV

PEACE

APP: *We can search for peace in many different ways and places. But it's tough to identify it and find it. It's more than good feelings or an action or positive thinking or a word you chant. Some might say it's freedom from arguments, stress, or fear. The world that we live in defines peace as lack of conflict. But peace isn't necessarily the absence of war. You could be in the middle of a fierce battle yet still be at peace. Or you could be chillin' on an amazing tropical island and lack peace because of things like uncertainty, fear, and doubt at war within you. Deep and lasting peace is a result of God at work in our lives. It's about a state of being—inner contentment and rest. God's peace gives us confidence and assurance no matter what we are experiencing. True peace gives us the ability to live without fear of the present or the future. We can't live in peace with others unless we are at peace with ourselves. And we can't be at peace with ourselves until we are at peace with God. Jesus will give us peace if we will accept it from Him.*

Do not be anxious about anything, but in every situation, by prayer and petition, with thanksgiving, present your requests to God. And the peace of God, which transcends all understanding, will guard your hearts and your minds in Christ Jesus.

PHILIPPIANS 4:6–7 NIV

Let the peace of Christ rule in your hearts, since as members of one body you were called to peace. And be thankful.

COLOSSIANS 3:15 NIV

You will keep in perfect peace those whose minds are steadfast, because they trust in you. Trust in the LORD forever, for the LORD, the LORD himself, is the Rock eternal.

ISAIAH 26:3–4 NIV

For unto us a Child is born, unto us a Son is given; and the government will be upon His shoulder. And His name will be called Wonderful, Counselor, Mighty God, Everlasting Father, Prince of Peace.

ISAIAH 9:6 NKJV

If possible, so far as it depends on you, be at peace with all men.
ROMANS 12:18 NASB

"Blessed are the peacemakers, for they will be called children of God."

MATTHEW 5:9 NIV

PEER PRESSURE

APP: *One of the biggest influences in our lives is peer pressure. It's the pressure we get from those around us to follow their way of thinking about life. For some this "force" from our friends can be so strong it becomes a sort of self-imposed prison. The pressure to conform tells us what we think about ourselves, parents, language, and lifestyle and even what we buy into as being right and wrong. But there's something subtle that motivates us to conform—the need for acceptance. Everyone wants to feel like they belong. The real fear is how far we will go to be accepted and what we will compromise to fit in. Our best defense to the problem of peer pressure is to become inner-directed rather than taking our guidance in life from outside. Not a lot of people really want to be chameleons that adapt to their surroundings just for survival. To be inner-directed we have to choose our friends carefully, develop a set of personal standards to live by based on a biblical worldview, know and understand who we are, and do what is right—not what is convenient.*

No temptation has overtaken you but such as is common to man; and God is faithful, who will not allow you to be tempted beyond what you are able, but with the temptation will provide the way of escape also, so that you will be able to endure it.

1 Corinthians 10:13 NASB

The world and its desires pass away, but whoever does the will of God lives forever.

1 John 2:17 NIV

Let no one deceive you with empty words, for because of such things God's wrath comes on those who are disobedient. Therefore do not be partners with them. For you were once darkness, but now you are light in the Lord. Live as children of light (for the fruit of the light consists in all goodness, righteousness and truth) and find out what pleases the Lord.

Ephesians 5:6–10 NIV

He who walks with wise men will be wise, but the companion of fools will suffer harm.

Proverbs 13:20 NASB

Do not be misled: "Bad company corrupts good character."

1 Corinthians 15:33 NIV

PERSECUTION

APP: *Persecution is dreadful. It's the organized mistreatment of an individual or group. It comes in many types, but the most common ones are political, religious, and ethnic. Throughout history millions have experienced maltreatment resulting in murder, extermination, enslavement, and other cruel acts committed against civilian populations. It's weird to think that it's still happening today when we are supposed to be living in an "age of tolerance."*

For centuries, those who follow Jesus have been tortured. Millions have been killed for their faith. This is something that comes with being a Christian. It shouldn't surprise you when others unfairly criticize you or they try to hurt you because of your beliefs and the way you live. Don't quit or give up. Instead, keep doing what you know is right and pleases God. Jesus said we should be happy when we're persecuted for our faith. Get real—that's not easy to do. Even though you may not totally understand why you are being abused for following Jesus, it's a good sign. It means that you are being faithful and making a difference. If you weren't, nobody would notice. And remember, God rewards those who remain faithful.

Indeed, all who desire to live godly in Christ Jesus will be persecuted.

2 TIMOTHY 3:12 NASB

"Blessed are you when *people* insult you and persecute you, and falsely say all kinds of evil against you because of Me [Jesus]. Rejoice and be glad, for your reward in heaven is great; for in the same way they persecuted the prophets who were before you."

MATTHEW 5:11–12 NASB

Bless those who persecute you. Don't curse them; pray that God will bless them.

ROMANS 12:14 NLT

"Blessed are those who are persecuted because of righteousness, for theirs is the kingdom of heaven."
MATTHEW 5:10 NIV

"If the world hates you, remember that it hated me [Jesus] first. The world would love you as one of its own if you belonged to it, but you are no longer part of the world. I chose you to come out of the world, so it hates you. Do you remember what I told you? 'A slave is not greater than the master.' Since they persecuted me, naturally they will persecute you. And if they had listened to me, they would listen to you."

JOHN 15:18–20 NLT

PORNOGRAPHY

APP: *Pornography is a huge problem today. It is one of the most searched topics online. Just about everybody's had a porn site pop up on their screen or accidently been diverted to one. What God designed to be good, right, and satisfying between a husband and a wife has been replaced. It's now been twisted and perverted into a lust-crazed form of visual entertainment. You begin to view people of the opposite sex as a means to satisfy an obsession. Pornography is extremely addictive, just like someone who abuses drugs. The "high" you get is very seductive and makes it easy for you to get dragged deeper and deeper into a sensual prison. There's no doubt pornography's offensive to God. He's the only One who has the power to free you from this addictive bondage. There are a couple of action steps if you really want to be free. The most important is to confess your sin, asking God to help you turn away from it. Ask Him to clean and transform your mind, filling it with pure thoughts. Also, you must stop putting yourself in a position where you have ready access to pornography. It may even involve installing porn-blockers on your computer.*

Each of you should learn to control your own body in a way that is holy and honorable, not in passionate lust like the pagans, who do not know God.

1 THESSALONIANS 4:4–5 NIV

God didn't choose you to be filthy, but to be pure.

1 THESSALONIANS 4:7 CEV

Put to death, therefore, whatever belongs to your earthly nature: sexual immorality, impurity, lust, evil desires and greed, which is idolatry. Because of these, the wrath of God is coming. You used to walk in these ways, in the life you once lived. But now you must also rid yourselves of all such things as these: anger, rage, malice, slander, and filthy language from your lips. Do not lie to each other, since you have taken off your old self with its practices and have put on the new self, which is being renewed in knowledge in the image of its Creator.

COLOSSIANS 3:5–10 NIV

God wants you to be holy, so don't be immoral in matters of sex.

1 THESSALONIANS 4:3 CEV

The acts of the flesh are obvious: sexual immorality, impurity and debauchery; idolatry and witchcraft; hatred, discord, jealousy, fits of rage, selfish ambition, dissensions, factions and envy; drunkenness, orgies, and the like. I warn you, as I did before, that those who live like this will not inherit the kingdom of God.

GALATIANS 5:19–21 NIV

POVERTY

APP: *Poverty is nothing new. It dates back to the beginning of human history, and it will continue until life as we know it on this planet ends. When you can't afford basic human needs like clean water, food, health care, clothing, shelter, and education, you're living in poverty. It sounds crazy, but there can actually be certain advantages to being poor. The most important benefit is recognizing that you have to totally depend on God for everything. He is the only One who can offer the escape you really want. You have the advantage of knowing that you are interdependent on others who share a similar situation. There's the benefit of recognizing that your security isn't in things but in other people. And you have the ability of distinguishing between what you want and what you need. Sometimes it's easy to want to avoid or ignore the poor. It's cooler to hang out with others who are wealthy and popular. God wants us to help and encourage the poor. We have to be willing to spend more time with the poor and outcasts of society. Even simple things like a drink of water or providing shelter can make a difference.*

Whoever disregards discipline comes to poverty and shame, but whoever heeds correction is honored.

PROVERBS 13:18 NIV

"So don't be afraid, little flock. For it gives your Father great happiness to give you the Kingdom. Sell your possessions and give to those in need. This will store up treasure for you in heaven! And the purses of heaven never get old or develop holes. Your treasure will be safe; no thief can steal it and no moth can destroy it. Wherever your treasure is, there the desires of your heart will also be."

LUKE 12:32–34 NLT

"The LORD sends poverty and wealth; he humbles and he exalts."
1 SAMUEL 2:7 NIV

The plans of the diligent lead to profit as surely as haste leads to poverty.

PROVERBS 21:5 NIV

He who oppresses the poor to make more for himself or who gives to the rich, *will* only *come to* poverty.

PROVERBS 22:16 NASB

For you know the grace of our Lord Jesus Christ, that though He was rich, yet for your sake He became poor, so that you through His poverty might become rich.

2 CORINTHIANS 8:9 NASB

POWER

APP: *Most people want power to improve their lives. Some want power to get what they want—whether it's bling, money, or even love. Others want to get vengeance on people who've hurt them. Some people think power represents glam and fame. Infomercial gurus claim that there's a hidden power deep within us that we need to learn how to develop. Others believe we can draw energy from nature. Practitioners use a wide variety of objects, such as crystals, stones, candles, and herbs. Some even make use of chants, spells, and poetry to gain power. This can all sound intriguing, but if we lack the power in ourselves to start with—to change our lives, help us cope, or whatever else the specific need might be—it's crazy to think that we'll be able to conjure up some untapped reservoir deep inside us. Holding a rock or crystal, chanting, burning colored candles, or even reciting poetry isn't going to help. The energy we need for living has to come from a source outside ourselves. The source of power must be bigger than us, and has to be unlimited. The source of this power is the living God. Have you looked at some of the characteristics of God described in the Bible that describe His limitless power that is able to overcome even the most insurmountable problems?*

For God has not given us a spirit of fear, but of power and of love and of a sound mind.

2 TIMOTHY 1:7 NKJV

Wisdom makes one wise person more powerful than ten rulers in a city.
ECCLESIASTES 7:19 NIV

A final word: Be strong in the Lord and in his mighty power. Put on all of God's armor so that you will be able to stand firm against all strategies of the devil.

EPHESIANS 6:10–11 NLT

"Yours, O LORD, is the greatness, the power, the glory, the victory, and the majesty. Everything in the heavens and on earth is yours, O LORD, and this is your kingdom. We adore you as the one who is over all things. Wealth and honor come from you alone, for you rule over everything. Power and might are in your hand, and at your discretion people are made great and given strength."

1 CHRONICLES 29:11–12 NLT

"But true wisdom and power are found in God; counsel and understanding are his."

JOB 12:13 NLT

PRAYER

APP: *Prayer has got to be the most misunderstood and underused part of our lives. Check this out: We have the amazing opportunity and privilege to talk personally with the Creator of the universe! We don't have to take a number and wait in line or make an appointment. He's available to us 24-7. . .365. God not only listens to us; He answers our prayers! Sometimes the answer is not what we expected or it doesn't happen when we think it should. But God always does what's best for us and at just the right time. He sees our entire lives—from beginning to end—and knows what we need and when we need it. Sometimes it's tough to trust God and wait for His answer. We live in an instant culture that demands gratification now. God's perspective is different because He is outside the boundaries of time and space. But it's difficult to trust someone whom you don't know at all or very well. Our confidence in prayer is going to grow in proportion to our relationship with God. The deeper our relationship with Him, the more faith we will have in the power of prayer.*

Save me, O God, by your name; vindicate me by your might. Hear my prayer, O God; listen to the words of my mouth.

PSALM 54:1–2 NIV

Do not be anxious about anything, but in every situation, by prayer and petition, with thanksgiving, present your requests to God. And the peace of God, which transcends all understanding, will guard your hearts and your minds in Christ Jesus.

PHILIPPIANS 4:6–7 NIV

Devote yourselves to prayer, being watchful and thankful.
COLOSSIANS 4:2 NIV

Is anyone among you in trouble? Let them pray. Is anyone happy? Let them sing songs of praise.

JAMES 5:13 NIV

"For the eyes of the Lord are on the righteous, and his ears are open to their prayer. But the face of the Lord is against those who do evil."

1 PETER 3:12 ESV

"But you, when you pray, go into your room, and when you have shut your door, pray to your Father who *is* in the secret *place*; and your Father who sees in secret will reward you openly."

MATTHEW 6:6 NKJV

PREJUDICE

APP: *Being prejudiced means you have locked into a belief, opinion, or judgment without getting all the facts about a person or situation. It can be because of race, gender, social class, age, ethnicity, or a disability. These unreasonable and uniformed attitudes can motivate you to act in certain ways that could even result in violence. Why should people be treated unequally just because they happen to belong to a certain people group? You can see tensions of prejudice and its effects revealed in many different forms nationally and internationally—from gang turf wars on the streets of Los Angeles to fighting in the Middle East. If only we could all have the eyes of a child. Children don't see the color of someone's skin or their social class. More importantly, we need to see people as God sees them. God loves every person the same. There's no one who is loved less or loved more because of skin color, age, or social class. God treats us all the same because we are all equal in Him. We can prevent prejudice one person at a time. It starts by simply being kind to one another.*

Then Peter began to speak: "I now realize how true it is that God does not show favoritism but accepts from every nation the one who fears him and does what is right."

ACTS 10:34–35 NIV

My brothers and sisters, believers in our glorious Lord Jesus Christ must not show favoritism.

JAMES 2:1 NIV

For you are all sons of God through faith in Christ Jesus. For as many of you as were baptized into Christ have put on Christ. There is neither Jew nor Greek, there is neither slave nor free, there is neither male nor female; for you are all one in Christ Jesus. And if you *are* Christ's, then you are Abraham's seed, and heirs according to the promise.

GALATIANS 3:26–29 NKJV

In this new life, it doesn't matter if you are a Jew or a Gentile, circumcised or uncircumcised, barbaric, uncivilized, slave, or free. Christ is all that matters, and he lives in all of us.

COLOSSIANS 3:11 NLT

"When a foreigner lives with you in your land, don't take advantage of him. Treat the foreigner the same as a native. Love him like one of your own. Remember that you were once foreigners in Egypt. I am GOD, your God."

LEVITICUS 19:33–34 MSG

PRIORITIES

APP: *Our calendars say a lot about us. Whether we use one on our smart phone or computer, they are a picture of what is really important to us. What matters most to you? Whatever is valuable to us will be reflected in our priorities. They're those things of main concern that help us manage our time wisely by establishing an order of importance. Sometimes priorities even give us a sense of urgency for things we do.*

We all have lots of opportunities every day that can be tempting and even distracting. But they're not all bad things. That's why it comes down to choosing carefully and not sweating the small stuff. Making the right choices can help us to keep going in the right direction and to stay focused. If we've made a decision to live for and like Jesus, our priorities will be different from those of others. Even though school, relationships, and a job for the future are all important, they would be lower on our list of priorities. Things like loving God and others, growing in character, having a good reputation, and serving God would be at the top of our list of main concerns.

"But if serving the Lord seems undesirable to you, then choose for yourselves this day whom you will serve, whether the gods your ancestors served beyond the Euphrates, or the gods of the Amorites, in whose land you are living. But as for me and my household, we will serve the Lord."

JOSHUA 24:15 NIV

Don't be obsessed with getting more material things. Be relaxed with what you have. Since God assured us, "I'll never let you down, never walk off and leave you," we can boldly quote, God is there, ready to help; I'm fearless no matter what. Who or what can get to me?

HEBREWS 13:5–6 MSG

So we fix our eyes not on what is seen, but on what is unseen, since what is seen is temporary, but what is unseen is eternal.

2 CORINTHIANS 4:18 NIV

"No one can serve two masters. Either you will hate the one and love the other, or you will be devoted to the one and despise the other. You cannot serve both God and money."

MATTHEW 6:24 NIV

Then Jesus said to His disciples, "If anyone desires to come after Me, let him deny himself, and take up his cross, and follow Me. For whoever desires to save his life will lose it, but whoever loses his life for My sake will find it."

MATTHEW 16:24–25 NKJV

PROBLEMS

APP: *How do you handle problems in your life? I'm not talking about the everyday ones, but the really big obstacles—the tough ones. Each situation, condition, or issue that is unresolved begs for an answer or solution. Everyone deals with problems, but the important thing is how we deal with them and who faces them with us. What is the greatest problem you face today? When we are facing problems that are so overwhelming that there seems to be no way out, we have to change our focus. Instead of concentrating on the problems, we should center our attention on God. By listening to Him, we can cut through the confusing voices all around us and see the problems for what they really are: opportunities for God to work in our lives. Once we start to understand what He wants from us in a situation, we have to obey Him. Chances are, it won't be easy, but if it comes from God, it will be the right thing to do. Sometimes we wonder if He will solve our problems. I know from my own experience that He can and will solve them any way He chooses to.*

Humble yourselves, therefore, under God's mighty hand, that he may lift you up in due time. Cast all your anxiety on him because he cares for you.

1 PETER 5:6–7 NIV

You who have shown me many troubles and distresses will revive me again, and will bring me up again from the depths of the earth.

PSALM 71:20 NASB

The righteous cry out, and the LORD hears them; he delivers them from all their troubles. The LORD is close to the brokenhearted and saves those who are crushed in spirit. The righteous person may have many troubles, but the LORD delivers him from them all; he protects all his bones, not one of them will be broken.

PSALM 34:17–20 NIV

"Can any one of you by worrying
add a single hour to your life?"
MATTHEW 6:27 NIV

"For I hold you by your right hand—I, the LORD your God. And I say to you, 'Don't be afraid. I am here to help you.'"

ISAIAH 41:13 NLT

PURPOSE IN LIFE

APP: *Our culture is full of roadblocks that get in the way of us finding meaning and purpose in life. It's easy to think that being popular or having money, fame, and possessions is what it takes to make life worth living. Just look at the celebs, rock stars, and pro athletes who seem totally satisfied with life. It may seem that way from the outside looking in, but it's not reality. Unfortunately, lots of people in the spotlight who have everything you think you could ever want or need are empty inside. They're still searching for a way to fill the emptiness deep inside and to make sense out of life. That's what happens when we ignore the One who created us and try to live without Him. God is the only One who can give us true meaning and purpose to our lives. Who would know better than the One who created us? His ultimate plan is to transform us so radically that we live for and like Jesus. Do you have a reason to get up in the morning? If your life lacks purpose, maybe it's because you're not allowing God to work in and through you.*

The Lord will vindicate me; your love, Lord, endures forever—do not abandon the works of your hands.

Psalm 138:8 niv

"Before I [God] shaped you in the womb, I knew all about you. Before you saw the light of day, I had holy plans for you: A prophet to the nations—that's what I had in mind for you."

Jeremiah 1:5 msg

Many are the plans in a person's heart, but it is the Lord's purpose that prevails.

Proverbs 19:21 niv

And we know that in all things God works for the good of those who love him, who have been called according to his purpose.

Romans 8:28 niv

"For I know the plans I have for you," declares the Lord, "plans to prosper you and not to harm you, plans to give you hope and a future."

Jeremiah 29:11 niv

RAPE

APP: *If sex is forced against someone's will, it's rape—one of the most wicked crimes ever committed. Rape isn't about love; it's an act of aggression and violence. Sexual sin like rape is devastating because its consequences are so far-reaching. Victims can sometimes deal with emotional and physical struggles for years. But the rapist will also face consequences of a different kind. Girls and women are most often victims of rape, but guys can be too. About half of all people who are raped know the person who attacked them. In some parts of the world today, rape and sexual slavery have become widespread organized practices. These brutal activities are recognized as crimes against humanity. Rape has also become an element of genocide when it's been used to try to destroy a selected ethnic group. No matter what kind of rape is committed—date, gang, prison, or statutory—it's hard to understand the motivation behind the crime. Rape is usually not about sexual satisfaction. Instead, the motivation could be more about anger, curiosity, money, blackmail, punishment, or a desire for power. God does not overlook rape. It is a dreadful and ugly sin.*

The LORD is close to the brokenhearted; he rescues those whose spirits are crushed.

PSALM 34:18 NLT

**"Peace I [Jesus] leave with you;
my peace I give you. I do not give to
you as the world gives. Do not let your
hearts be troubled and do not be afraid."**
JOHN 14:27 NIV

Cast your burden upon the LORD and He will sustain you; He will never allow the righteous to be shaken.

PSALM 55:22 NASB

It is God's will that you should be sanctified: that you should avoid sexual immorality; that each of you should learn to control your own body in a way that is holy and honorable, not in passionate lust like the pagans, who do not know God; and that in this matter no one should wrong or take advantage of a brother or sister. The Lord will punish all those who commit such sins, as we told you and warned you before.

1 THESSALONIANS 4:3–6 NIV

The LORD is my strength and my shield; my heart trusts in him, and he helps me. My heart leaps for joy, and with my song I praise him.

PSALM 28:7 NIV

REBELLION

APP: *Rebellion goes down when you refuse to accept an authority or a set of rules. It could be on a larger scale or personal. Throughout human history there has been "civil disobedience" and organized attempts to destroy established authorities like dictators or governments. Personal rebellion can also be against governmental systems. In addition, it can be against parents and sometimes even God. It's not unusual to put off advice from our parents when we're trying to develop an independent identity from them and shape our own values. This search is kind of experimental as we look at different roles and activities. And it can also involve risk-taking. This kind of rebellion isn't necessarily bad. Neither is rebelling against the status quo in society in search of positive change. The rebellion we have to be careful of is against God. A negative attitude can be the first quiet step. We get discouraged and start grumbling. We're dissatisfied and skeptical about God. Our faith begins to erode, we complain about our circumstances, and we become bitter. Pretty soon we think we can make it through life without God. Choosing to side against Him is never a smart move.*

Do not enter the path of the wicked and do not proceed in the way of evil men.

PROVERBS 4:14 NASB

"For rebellion is like the sin of divination, and arrogance like the evil of idolatry."

1 SAMUEL 15:23 NIV

Whoever scorns instruction will pay for it, but whoever respects a command is rewarded.

PROVERBS 13:13 NIV

If you reject discipline, you only harm yourself; but if you listen to correction, you grow in understanding.

PROVERBS 15:32 NLT

But rebels and sinners will be completely destroyed, and those who desert the LORD will be consumed.

ISAIAH 1:28 NLT

My child, fear the LORD and the king. Don't associate with rebels, for disaster will hit them suddenly. Who knows what punishment will come from the LORD and the king?

PROVERBS 24:21–22 NLT

RELATIONSHIPS

APP: *No one is an island. We weren't designed to go at life solo; we need each other. Our lives are a complicated web of relationships at home, at school, at work, in our community, and even online through social networks. Just think about all the kinds of relationships that you have, from friends to parents. Because we're human and interact on so many different levels, we're bound to experience problems and drama from time to time. When this happens there's no shortage of places to go for advice. From Oprah to Dr. Phil to faceless blogs—lots of people are only too glad to share their opinions with us. While some of this advice may seem helpful, the best place we can go for guidance is God's Word. Who better to give us advice on how to get along with others than the One who created each one of us? The Bible has solid advice that we can trust to be helpful and practical. But sometimes the toughest part is taking "me" out of the picture and looking at things from another point of view. Listen carefully to what God has to say, and then do it.*

Above all, love each other deeply, because love covers over a multitude of sins.

1 PETER 4:8 NIV

So let's stop condemning each other. Decide instead to live in such a way that you will not cause another believer to stumble and fall.

ROMANS 14:13 NLT

As iron sharpens iron, so one person sharpens another.
PROVERBS 27:17 NIV

Two are better than one because they have a good return for their labor. For if either of them falls, the one will lift up his companion. But woe to the one who falls when there is not another to lift him up.

ECCLESIASTES 4:9–10 NASB

Love is patient, love is kind. It does not envy, it does not boast, it is not proud. It does not dishonor others, it is not self-seeking, it is not easily angered, it keeps no record of wrongs. Love does not delight in evil but rejoices with the truth. It always protects, always trusts, always hopes, always perseveres. Love never fails.

1 CORINTHIANS 13:4–8 NIV

Owe nothing to anyone except to love one another; for he who loves his neighbor has fulfilled *the* law.

ROMANS 13:8 NASB

RESPECT

APP: *When we give respect to someone (parent, friend, God, etc.) or something (country, flag, law, etc.), it means we are showing appreciation and high regard. It's a powerful word of value that we place in a person or thing. We demonstrate our respect in different ways, including our words, actions, and attitudes. It's like when we pledge allegiance to the flag; we hold our hands over our hearts out of respect for what it represents. It can be hard to respect others if we don't respect ourselves. When we understand how God values us, we'll be able to respect ourselves and others. Respect is a theme that's found throughout the Bible. God wants us to treat everyone we meet with respect—even when we feel like they don't deserve it—because everyone is created in His image. There will be times when we end up respecting the position someone has rather than the person because we disagree with their actions. However, God is always deserving and worthy of our respect. Even though God is our friend, we shouldn't approach Him casually, but as if we've been invited to have an audience with a king—the God of creation.*

Show proper respect to everyone, love the family of believers, fear God, honor the emporer.

1 PETER 2:17 NIV

**Give to everyone what you owe them:
Pay your taxes and government fees to
those who collect them, and give respect
and honor to those who are in authority.**
ROMANS 13:7 NLT

"Each of you must show great respect for your mother and father, and you must always observe my Sabbath days of rest. I am the LORD your God."

LEVITICUS 19:3 NLT

"Stand up in the presence of the aged, show respect for the elderly and revere your God. I am the LORD."

LEVITICUS 19:32 NIV

Whoever scorns instruction will pay for it, but whoever respects a command is rewarded.

PROVERBS 13:13 NIV

RESURRECTION

APP: *Only Christianity has a God who became a man, died on a cross for all people, and came back to life. Jesus is alive; all other religious leaders are dead. Without the resurrection, everything else about Christianity becomes meaningless, including the death of Christ. The empty tomb is a guarantee to us that all the things that Jesus taught are true. To fully get the importance of the resurrection, we have to clearly define it. The resurrection talked about in the Bible is physical, not spiritual. The word* resurrection *literally means the "standing up of a corpse." What an awesome promise! Think about it. One day our dead bodies are going to "stand up" from the grave!*

The amazing thing about the Christian faith is that we never view death as the end. Instead, we look into eternity and see the hope that is offered through the resurrected life of Jesus Christ. Because Jesus has risen from the grave, we can have a personal relationship with the living God. Today He uses the same power that raised Jesus from the grave to radically transform our lives. Have you been changed? Is the resurrection power a reality in your life?

Jesus said to her, "I am the resurrection and the life. The one who believes in me will live, even though they die; and whoever lives by believing in me will never die. Do you believe this?"

JOHN 11:25–26 NIV

By his power God raised the Lord from the dead, and he will raise us also.

1 CORINTHIANS 6:14 NIV

If only for this life we have hope in Christ, we are of all people most to be pitied. But Christ has indeed been raised from the dead, the firstfruits of those who have fallen asleep. For since death came through a man, the resurrection of the dead comes also through a man. For as in Adam all die, so in Christ all will be made alive.

1 CORINTHIANS 15:19–22 NIV

I will explain a mystery to you. Not every one of us will die, but we will all be changed. It will happen suddenly, quicker than the blink of an eye. At the sound of the last trumpet the dead will be raised. We will all be changed, so that we will never die again. Our dead and decaying bodies will be changed into bodies that won't die or decay. The bodies we now have are weak and can die. But they will be changed into bodies that are eternal. Then the Scriptures will come true, "Death has lost the battle! Where is its victory? Where is its sting?" Sin is what gives death its sting, and the Law is the power behind sin. But thank God for letting our Lord Jesus Christ give us the victory!

1 CORINTHIANS 15:51–57 CEV

SACRIFICE

APP: *God's view of sacrifice is different from a short-term loss in return for a greater gain—like a batter does in a baseball game when he hits a sacrifice bunt. And things have changed in a big way from biblical times when animals were sacrificed as an act of worship to please God. Even by performing selfless good deeds for others, you are missing the real point of how God views sacrifice. His desire for you is to be a living sacrifice. God wants you to offer yourself to Him, not animals. It's about obedience more than practicing some religious ritual or tradition. And sacrifice is not just giving up something you would rather keep. Being a living sacrifice is laying aside our desires each day in order to follow God. We hand over all of our energy and resources for Him to use as He pleases, trusting that He'll guide us. What gives God the right to ask for this kind of sacrifice from you and me? Because of the ultimate sacrifice He made on our behalf when His only Son, Jesus, died our death and paid our sin debt on the cross. It's gratitude that our sins have been forgiven that motivates us to daily surrender our lives.*

Therefore, let us offer through Jesus a continual sacrifice of praise to God, proclaiming our allegiance to his name.

HEBREWS 13:15 NLT

This is real love—not that we loved God, but that he loved us and sent his Son [Jesus] as a sacrifice to take away our sins.

1 JOHN 4:10 NLT

He [Jesus] is the atoning sacrifice for our sins, and not only for ours but also for the sins of the whole world.

1 JOHN 2:2 NIV

Follow God's example, therefore, as dearly loved children and walk in the way of love, just as Christ loved us and gave himself up for us as a fragrant offering and sacrifice to God.
EPHESIANS 5:1–2 NIV

And do not forget to do good and to share with others, for with such sacrifices God is pleased.

HEBREWS 13:16 NIV

SALVATION

APP: *God acted on our behalf in an awesome way to save us from spiritual death so that we could experience eternal life. He accomplished this through the death, burial, and resurrection of His Son, Jesus Christ. Salvation is a free gift from God. There is absolutely nothing we can do to earn it or buy it. All of our efforts, such as doing good things, practicing traditions, being moral, performing acts of service, or even making intelligent choices are not enough to rescue us from the punishment for our sin. The only way we can receive this gift from God is by putting our faith and trust in Jesus. This act of surrender enables us to be brought back into a personal relationship with God. At salvation we also receive every good gift that God intends to give us—things like forgiveness, a place in His family, hope, peace, and a new power for living. Receiving these kinds of amazing gifts should cause us to be grateful for what God has given us. This gratitude should then motivate us to show our appreciation to God by serving Him through acts of service and kindness toward others.*

The LORD is my light and my salvation—whom shall I fear? The LORD is the stronghold of my life—of whom shall I be afraid?

PSALM 27:1 NIV

**Truly my soul finds rest in God;
my salvation comes from him.**
PSALM 62:1 NIV

For the message of the cross is foolishness to those who are perishing, but to us who are being saved it is the power of God.

1 CORINTHIANS 1:18 NIV

For by grace you have been saved through faith, and that not of yourselves; *it is* the gift of God, not of works, lest anyone should boast. For we are His workmanship, created in Christ Jesus for good works, which God prepared beforehand that we should walk in them.

EPHESIANS 2:8–10 NKJV

"For God so loved the world that He gave His only begotten Son, that whoever believes in Him should not perish but have everlasting life."

JOHN 3:16 NKJV

But God demonstrates his own love for us in this: While we were still sinners, Christ died for us.

ROMANS 5:8 NIV

SATISFACTION

APP: *Satisfaction is that "aha" experience we all feel when we have fulfilled a desire, a need, or an expectation. It's really about gratifying a hunger that could be physical, emotional, or spiritual. In our seductive and impulse-gratifying culture, we are bombarded with images of things we are supposed to want. It's easy to fall into the trap and let the urge consume us until we get what we want. At first we have this extreme feeling of being really satisfied because we got what we thought we had to have. But immediate pleasure doesn't satisfy. It loses sight of the future. Learning to compare short-term pleasure with long-term consequences is a good thing. We can't let the pressure or temptation of the moment warp our view of future consequences. This can easily happen when we buy the lie that tells us we are dissatisfied with what we have and our concentration shifts to what we don't have. When we take things for granted, we can become ungrateful for all that God has given us. Satisfaction and purpose are tied together. That's why only a personal relationship with God will satisfy those desires we have deep inside. It's contentment that lasts.*

"Blessed are those who hunger and thirst for righteousness, for they shall be satisfied."

MATTHEW 5:6 ESV

So I decided there is nothing better than to enjoy food and drink and to find satisfaction in work. Then I realized that these pleasures are from the hand of God.

ECCLESIASTES 2:24 NLT

Pay careful attention to your own work, for then you will get the satisfaction of a job well done, and you won't need to compare yourself to anyone else.

GALATIANS 6:4 NLT

"The LORD will guide you always; he will satisfy your needs in a sun-scorched land and will strengthen your frame. You will be like a well-watered garden, like a spring whose waters never fail."

ISAIAH 58:11 NIV

SELF-CONTROL

APP: *Having the ability to control our emotions, desires, and actions is huge. It affects our lives today and in the future. To have self-control means we have the ability to deny ourselves and live within limits. It's something we all need. An out-of-control life opens us up to all sorts of attacks and crazy things. But self-control acts as a wall of defense and protection. It enables us to walk away from temptation. When we have self-control, we can master our moods and hold back our reactions to people and situations. It helps us stick to our schedule, handle our money, and stay healthy. Self-control also helps us to watch our words that can so easily cut and destroy others. Controlling our tongues is a good place to start developing self-control. It's as simple as stopping to think before we speak. The cool thing is, if we can control this small part of our body, we can manage the rest. Check out other areas of your life to see where you are lacking control and do something about them. But remember, developing self-control isn't something that we can do on our own. We need supernatural power—God's—to make it happen in our lives.*

Like a city whose walls are broken through is a person who lacks self-control.

PROVERBS 25:28 NIV

Our old self was crucified with *Him* [Jesus], in order that our body of sin might be done away with, so that we would no longer be slaves to sin.

ROMANS 6:6 NASB

But the fruit of the Spirit is love, joy, peace, patience, kindness, goodness, faithfulness, gentleness, self-control; against such things there is no law.
GALATIANS 5:22–23 NASB

An undisciplined, self-willed life is puny; an obedient, God-willed life is spacious.

PROVERBS 15:32 MSG

The Law of the Lord is a lamp, and its teachings shine brightly. Correction and self-control will lead you through life.

PROVERBS 6:23 CEV

SELF-IMAGE

APP: *Self-image is a like a self-portrait. It's an internal dictionary that others have contributed to and describes characteristics about us. Our parents make one of the biggest contributions to our self-image, followed by friends, teachers, and extended family members. We continue to learn as we add to this "portrait dictionary." Information is taken in on a daily basis from others, our culture, and media that cause us to evaluate and compare. Our self-image is important, because what we think about ourselves directly affects how we feel about ourselves. This determines the quality of relationships we have with others. It also influences the way we react or respond to real-life stuff. Self-image has a big impact on us, but it doesn't necessarily reflect the truth about the "real us." How God sees us and how we view ourselves in Him are what's most important. When we discover our identity in Jesus, we can stop comparing ourselves to others and celebrate our own "uniqueness." Each one of us has a different set of gifts, talents, and abilities that are distinctively ours. A better way to look at self-image is to view it as Christ-image—who we are in Him. When this happens it will influence every part of our lives.*

I will give thanks to You, for I am fearfully and won-
derfully made; wonderful are Your works, and my
soul knows it very well.

PSALM 139:14 NASB

But the LORD said to Samuel, "Do not look on his
appearance or on the height of his stature, because I
have rejected him. For the LORD sees not as man sees:
man looks on the outward appearance, but the LORD
looks on the heart."

1 SAMUEL 16:7 ESV

Do not let your adorning be external—the braiding
of hair and the putting on of gold jewelry, or the
clothing you wear—but let your adorning be the
hidden person of the heart with the imperishable
beauty of a gentle and quiet spirit, which in God's
sight is very precious.

1 PETER 3:3–4 ESV

**For we are God's masterpiece. He has created
us anew in Christ Jesus, so we can do the
good things he planned for us long ago.**
EPHESIANS 2:10 NLT

Therefore, if anyone is in Christ, the new creation has
come: The old has gone, the new is here!

2 CORINTHIANS 5:17 NIV

SERVING

APP: *Serving God and others is at the center of our purpose for living. God has given us all tons of opportunities to serve. We become aware of the place and opportunity to serve when we turn our focus around—stop looking inside and start looking outside of ourselves. Serving involves taking risks and getting out of the zone that we so easily retreat to. There are many ways to serve others who are unable to do things for themselves. Some are big, while others are smaller. But they are all significant. There is power in simply serving others. It changes them and us. The world wants us to think it takes power to influence others. Jesus proved just the opposite. He's our example of what it means to serve. Be careful of hiding behind a list of excuses to obey God and serve. It's easy to get hung up on our own weaknesses and limitations. We fail to see how God can work through us. God has called each one of us to serve in specific ways. He promises to give us the tools and the strength we need. God is more concerned about our availability than our abilities.*

Each of you should use whatever gift you have received to serve others, as faithful stewards of God's grace in its various forms.

1 PETER 4:10 NIV

"In all things I have shown you that by working hard in this way we must help the weak and remember the words of the Lord Jesus, how he himself said, 'It is more blessed to give than to receive.' "

ACTS 20:35 ESV

[Jesus]. . .said, "Whoever wants to be first must take last place and be the servant of everyone else."

MARK 9:35 NLT

"Give, and it will be given to you. A good measure, pressed down, shaken together and running over, will be poured into your lap. For with the measure you use, it will be measured to you."

LUKE 6:38 NIV

"Whoever wishes to be first among you shall be slave of all. For even the Son of Man did not come to be served, but to serve, and to give His life a ransom for many."

MARK 10:44–45 NASB

You must each decide in your heart how much to give. And don't give reluctantly or in response to pressure. "For God loves a person who gives cheerfully."

2 CORINTHIANS 9:7 NLT

SEX / SEXUAL IMMORALITY

APP: *We live in a sex-crazed culture. It's everywhere and sells everything from vitamins to cars. The Internet has made porn readily available to anyone online. There has never been so much pressure to perform or indulge in perversion. If it's not "friends with benefits," it's "sexting." Growing numbers of guys and girls are sending highly suggestive and sexually explicit messages back and forth to each other. It usually starts casually in hopes that it will end in a sexual encounter. Popular culture lacks moral absolutes or any kind of sexual morality code. Consequences aren't considered until it's too late. At some point we all have to decide what we will do with the sexual dimension of our lives. God's perspective on sex is totally different from our culture. In the Bible, He helps us to understand that sexual immorality is the only sin we commit against ourselves. God also gives us guidelines for the role of sexuality in human interactions as it was designed to be. God created sex as a good thing to be enjoyed between a man and a woman through the commitment of marriage. It is the most amazing and intimate way to express love for one's spouse.*

Let marriage be held in honor among all, and let the marriage bed be undefiled, for God will judge the sexually immoral and adulterous.

HEBREWS 13:4 ESV

Run from sexual sin! No other sin so clearly affects the body as this one does. For sexual immorality is a sin against your own body.
1 CORINTHIANS 6:18 NLT

"But I tell you that anyone who looks at a woman lustfully has already committed adultery with her in his heart."

MATTHEW 5:28 NIV

It is God's will that you should be sanctified: that you should avoid sexual immorality; that each of you should learn to control your own body in a way that is holy and honorable, not in passionate lust like the pagans, who do not know God.

1 THESSALONIANS 4:3-5 NIV

But because of the temptation to sexual immorality, each man should have his own wife and each woman her own husband.

1 CORINTHIANS 7:2 ESV

SIN

APP: *Sin is an outdated-sounding word that doesn't seem to fit in our everyday talk. It's hard to get a handle on this idea in a culture where right and wrong no longer seem to exist. Is it lying to your parents? Cheating on a test? Killing somebody? Or how about refusing to be nice to another person? All of these things are sins in God's eyes. The Bible describes sin in several ways, including falling short of God's standards, knowing what the right thing to do is and not doing it, rebelling against God, and even having the wrong motivation for doing something that outwardly appears to be good. At its very core, sin is trying to live your life without God—independent from Him. It is a spiritual terminal disease that we inherited from the first man and woman—Adam and Eve. Being a follower of Jesus doesn't mean we stop sinning. Instead, it means our heart is shredded because we realize how intensely our sins hurt God and create a humongous gap between us and our Father in heaven. God loves us and forgives us. And He gives us the power to live free from sin's control over us. Does your sin bother you enough to ask God to forgive and help you?*

But if we live in the light, as God does, we share in life with each other. And the blood of his Son Jesus washes all our sins away.

1 JOHN 1:7 CEV

O God, you know my folly; the wrongs I have done are not hidden from you.

PSALM 69:5 ESV

But God shows his love for us in that while we were still sinners, Christ died for us.
ROMANS 5:8 ESV

But if we confess our sins, he will forgive our sins, because we can trust God to do what is right. He will cleanse us from all the wrongs we have done.

1 JOHN 1:9 NCV

For the wages of sin is death, but the free gift of God is eternal life through Christ Jesus our Lord.

ROMANS 6:23 NLT

For all have sinned and fall short of the glory of God.

ROMANS 3:23 NKJV

Remember, it is sin to know what you ought to do and then not do it.

JAMES 4:17 NLT

SPIRITUAL GIFTS

APP: *God gives us special gifts to build up His church and serve others. Not everyone has the same gift or combination of gifts. They're given in a way to balance each other's strengths and weaknesses. A variety of gifts are listed in the Bible, including teaching, giving, compassion, discernment, wisdom, encouragement, and evangelism. Because they're given to us by God, we shouldn't use them for our own personal success. Spiritual gifts and abilities are different from the fruits of the Spirit. Gifts are given to us to be used, while spiritual fruits are character traits of living a Spirit-controlled life. We should ask God to show us how and where He wants us to use our gifts. That's why it's important to know the specific abilities that God has given us. Spiritual gifts are a huge topic. Think about what could be accomplished to change the world if we all got serious about using our gifts—with all our heart—to serve God and others. God has an amazing plan to use each of us to make a difference with our lives. If we are faithful to obey and surrender our gifts to Him, He will equip and use us.*

In his grace, God has given us different gifts for doing certain things well. So if God has given you the ability to prophesy, speak out with as much faith as God has given you. If your gift is serving others, serve them well. If you are a teacher, teach well. If your gift is to encourage others, be encouraging. If it is giving, give generously. If God has given you leadership ability, take the responsibility seriously. And if you have a gift for showing kindness to others, do it gladly.

ROMANS 12:6–8 NLT

And Christ gave gifts to people—he made some to be apostles, some to be prophets, some to go and tell the Good News, and some to have the work of caring for and teaching God's people.
EPHESIANS 4:11 NCV

There are different kinds of spiritual gifts, but the same Spirit is the source of them all. There are different kinds of service, but we serve the same Lord. God works in different ways, but it is the same God who does the work in all of us.

1 CORINTHIANS 12:4–6 NLT

Just as each of us has one body with many members, and these members do not all have the same function, so in Christ we, though many, form one body, and each member belongs to all the others.

ROMANS 12:4–5 NIV

SPIRITUAL WARFARE

APP: *We're all soldiers in a spiritual war. We're fighting in an intense, unseen battle against a very real enemy. The war includes such things as loneliness; lack of purpose; physical, verbal, and sexual abuse; addictions; premarital sex; abortion; broken families; eating disorders; gangs; and suicide. It's a battle for our minds and emotions against the forces of darkness. The one who is behind much of this pain is relentless and a brilliant strategist. Satan's main objective is to devour and destroy. Without a doubt, it's the most crucial battle ever fought. And it's not something we can opt out of. But we do have a decision to make about how we will function in the war. The first choice has to do with who we're going to take orders from. Will our commander be Jesus or the devil? The second choice has to do with our weapons. Will we decide to use human weapons or God-given spiritual ones in combat? Because the devil never exercises a cease-fire in the war, we have to be continually on the alert for an attack. God has done an amazing job of giving us everything we need to win the war. It's up to us to decide to report for duty, ready to follow Jesus.*

For we do not wrestle against flesh and blood, but against the rulers, against the authorities, against the cosmic powers over this present darkness, against the spiritual forces of evil in the heavenly places.

EPHESIANS 6:12 ESV

We do live in the world, but we do not fight in the same way the world fights. We fight with weapons that are different from those the world uses. Our weapons have power from God that can destroy the enemy's strong places. We destroy people's arguments and every proud thing that raises itself against the knowledge of God. We capture every thought and make it give up and obey Christ.

2 CORINTHIANS 10:3–5 NCV

Put on God's whole armor [the armor of a heavy-armed soldier which God supplies], that you may be able successfully to stand up against [all] the strategies *and* the deceits of the devil.

EPHESIANS 6:11 AMPC

Surrender to God! Resist the devil, and he will run from you.

JAMES 4:7 CEV

Satan himself masquerades as an angel of light.

2 CORINTHIANS 11:14 AMPC

For the weapons of our warfare are not of the flesh but have divine power to destroy strongholds.

2 CORINTHIANS 10:4 ESV

SORCERY (see also Witchcraft)

APP: *Sorcery is not about fantasy or fairy tales. It's not a game but real-world stuff that actually works. At its very core, it is the desire to manipulate and control people, situations, and events. Those who practice sorcery believe in magick spells that can harness occult forces or evil spirits to produce unnatural effects in the natural world. They are encouraged to be creative, innovative, and show initiative. Magick is spelled with a k to distinguish the belief in using the universe's energy for spiritual purposes from the magical illusions performed by entertainers.*

To practice sorcery requires utilizing the darker powers instead of relying on the living God. And there's no end to the resources available for anyone who wants to perform sorcery. You can find online classes, books, articles, DVDs, apprenticeships, and even partnerships of multiple kinds. It's all about possessing the power to help you gain peace, success, wealth, love, and happiness. But the plan is to accomplish all of this outside of God's Word and His will. You must leave Him totally out of the equation. But any time you try to go it alone— without God—leaves you open for all kinds of not-so-positive consequences.

And when the people [instead of putting their trust in God] shall say to you, Consult for direction mediums and wizards who chirp and mutter, should not a people seek *and* consult their God? Should they consult the dead on behalf of the living?

ISAIAH 8:19 AMPC

"Do not turn to mediums or necromancers; do not seek them out, and so make yourselves unclean by them: I am the LORD your God."

LEVITICUS 19:31 ESV

**"There shall not be found among you
anyone who makes his son or his daughter
pass through the fire, *or one* who practices
witchcraft, *or* a soothsayer, or one who
interprets omens, or a sorcerer."
DEUTERONOMY 18:10 NKJV**

The LORD All-Powerful, the God of Israel, says: "Don't let the prophets among you and the people who do magic fool you. Don't listen to their dreams."

JEREMIAH 29:8 NCV

SUCCESS

APP: *Have you figured out what success means to you? It can mean a lot of different things to different people. Success and satisfaction are tied pretty close together. For some it means having money, popularity, and status. A lot of it depends on whose standards we are using to measure success, what lenses we are looking through to target our goals. Looking through the lenses of our culture versus biblical ones is enormously different. When God measures success it revolves around our personal relationship with Him. Success involves obedience and faithfulness. It's about accomplishing His purposes and goals for our lives.*

Sometimes looking at success through God's lenses will look like failure in the lenses of our culture. Take, for example, the story of Jeremiah from the Old Testament. This guy was seen as an absolute failure by his peers. For forty years Jeremiah was a spokesman for God. Trouble was, when he spoke, no one listened or responded. He was poor, thrown in prison, and rejected. But God saw him as a success because Jeremiah was faithful and accomplished God's purpose. Whatever success we do end up experiencing, we have to remember to give God the credit.

I can do all things through him who strengthens me.

PHILIPPIANS 4:13 ESV

"This Book of the Law shall not depart from your mouth, but you shall meditate in it day and night, that you may observe to do according to all that is written in it. For then you will make your way prosperous, and then you will have good success."

JOSHUA 1:8 NKJV

Wisdom brings success.

ECCLESIASTES 10:10 NKJV

"Then you will have success if you are careful to observe the decrees and laws that the LORD gave . . . Be strong and courageous. Do not be afraid or discouraged."

1 CHRONICLES 22:13 NIV

Commit your works to the LORD and your plans will be established.

PROVERBS 16:3 NASB

Respect and serve the LORD! Your reward will be wealth, a long life, and honor.

PROVERBS 22:4 CEV

SUFFERING

APP: *You can't escape suffering. It's something every one of us will go through at some time in our lives. Some of us will experience it more than others. We can end up suffering because of dumb choices we've made or as a result of someone else's wicked actions, like child abuse or genocide. Suffering can also happen when it's no one's fault, as with a natural disaster or an illness. We're not the first ones to struggle with suffering, and we won't be the last. It can touch us at the very core of our being. But God has a purpose in it. Because we are finite, we won't always be able to understand what's happening. By faith we can accept that God, being infinite, has what's best for us in mind. Being close to God will not keep us from suffering but will enable us to get through it. Hard times can be a form of discipline used by God when something needs to be tweaked in our lives. But most of the time God uses suffering to help us to grow and develop spiritually. We have to decide if we're going to become better instead of bitter. Attitude is huge. How we respond to suffering will reflect what we believe.*

And after you have suffered a little while, the God of all grace [Who imparts all blessing and favor], Who has called you to His [own] eternal glory in Christ *Jesus*, will Himself complete *and* make you what you ought to be, establish *and* ground you securely, and strengthen, and settle you.

1 PETER 5:10 AMPC

My brothers and sisters, when you have many kinds of troubles, you should be full of joy, because you know that these troubles test your faith, and this will give you patience. Let your patience show itself perfectly in what you do. Then you will be perfect and complete and will have everything you need.

JAMES 1:2–4 NCV

So then, since Christ suffered physical pain, you must arm yourselves with the same attitude he had, and be ready to suffer, too. For if you have suffered physically for Christ, you have finished with sin.

1 PETER 4:1 NLT

The sufferings we have now are nothing compared to the great glory that will be shown to us.

ROMANS 8:18 NCV

SUICIDE

APP: *Persons destroying themselves—and at times others—on purpose has become a global issue. We hear about suicide attacks by terrorists or a mass suicide by members of a cult. Sometimes two or more people agree on a plan to die together or separately in a suicide pact. Mostly we hear about individuals who feel that life isn't worth living anymore, so they end it. Maybe it's a friend at school who feels as if their problems are too big to handle or that no one really cares.*

Suicide is a permanent solution to a temporary problem. That's not to minimize agonizing problems that someone may be experiencing. But no matter how bad things may get in life, we need to realize that we can get through them. There are people in our lives who love us and care about us whom we can lean on. Jesus wants us to live an amazing life of meaning and purpose. He promises to help us through even the darkest of times. God's ultimate plan for us is life not death. Our lives belong to God. He bought us at a price—Jesus' death on the cross. It's never right to take our lives or someone else's. Hope is in the living God.

Do you not know that you are God's temple and that God's Spirit dwells in you?

1 CORINTHIANS 3:16 ESV

For God's temple is holy, and you are that temple.

1 CORINTHIANS 3:17 ESV

God paid a great price for you. So use your body to honor God.

1 CORINTHIANS 6:20 CEV

And we know that in all things God works for the good of those who love him, who have been called according to his purpose.
ROMANS 8:28 NIV

Surely you know that your bodies are parts of Christ himself.

1 CORINTHIANS 6:15 NCV

If I continue living in my body, I will be able to work for the Lord. I do not know what to choose—living or dying. It is hard to choose between the two. I want to leave this life and be with Christ, which is much better, but you need me here in my body. Since I am sure of this, I know I will stay with you to help you grow and have joy in your faith.

PHILIPPIANS 1:22–25 NCV

TATTOOS

APP: *Tattooing is practiced worldwide and dates back to the fourth and fifth centuries. Sometimes it's used to brand or identify animals, but we mainly know it as body mod on people. "Tats" or "ink" is really an art form that has become so popular that even mainstream art galleries are holding exhibitions. Depending on where you live, tattoos serve a lot of different purposes. They can be rites of passage, marks of status and rank, symbols of religious and spiritual devotion, decorations for bravery, pledges of love, and punishment. They can symbolize membership in a gang or be used cosmetically for permanent makeup. In World War II people were forcibly tattooed during the Holocaust. Most commonly today they are a way of expressing oneself.*

In the Christian community there are different opinions about tattoos. That's why it's important for us to know what the Bible actually teaches about tattoos and not try to twist passages from the Bible to say something that supports our position on whether Christ followers should or should not have them. Since there is no definitive answer, this is one area where we have to "agree to disagree" with others who don't share our opinion.

You surely know that your body is a temple where the Holy Spirit lives. The Spirit is in you and is a gift from God. You are no longer your own. God paid a great price for you. So use your body to honor God.

1 Corinthians 6:19–20 cev

Do you not know that you are the temple of God and *that* the Spirit of God dwells in you?

1 Corinthians 3:16 nkjv

I praise you because you made me in an amazing and wonderful way. What you have done is wonderful. I know this very well.

Psalm 139:14 ncv

Do not be conformed to this world, but be transformed by the renewal of your mind, that by testing you may discern what is the will of God, what is good and acceptable and perfect.
Romans 12:2 esv

"Do not cut your bodies for the dead, and do not mark your skin with tattoos. I am the Lord."

Leviticus 19:28 nlt

TEMPTATION

APP: *When you see a sign that says* DON'T TOUCH *or* NO, *do you suddenly feel an urge inside to lay a hand on it anyway? It's weird, but we are wired to give in to temptation. Advertisers spend a ton of money to make their products look more appealing than they really are. Temptation can be anything that draws us in, excites us, and seduces us. We usually think of temptation in a negative way because it can lead us to do something that we will end up wishing we hadn't done. Some people want to blame God for tempting them and for the consequences. He may test us, but God will never tempt anyone. The only one we have to blame when we give in to temptation is ourselves.*

But God does guarantee that He will never allow temptation in our lives to go too far. He also will uniquely mold the intensity of the attraction and escape route for each person. And God has given us an awesome tool—the Bible—to beat temptation. But for this to work effectively, scripture has to become an important part of our lives. Instead of getting pulled into temptation, get into God's Word.

No temptation has overtaken you that is not common to man. God is faithful, and he will not let you be tempted beyond your ability, but with the temptation he will also provide the way of escape, that you may be able to endure it.

1 Corinthians 10:13 esv

So be subject to God. Resist the devil [stand firm against him], and he will flee from you.
James 4:7 ampc

"Watch and pray that you may not enter into temptation. The spirit indeed is willing, but the flesh is weak."

Matthew 26:41 esv

Put on all of God's armor so that you will be able to stand firm against all strategies of the devil.

Ephesians 6:11 nlt

Do not set foot on the path of the wicked or walk in the way of evildoers. Avoid it, do not travel on it; turn from it and go on your way.

Proverbs 4:14–15 niv

You, dear children, are from God and have overcome them, because the one who is in you is greater than the one who is in the world.

1 John 4:4 niv

TOLERANCE

APP: *There's a ton of talk about tolerance today. It's a hot topic on every campus, in the news, and in the courts. Tolerance is a frontline culture battle for those living alternative lifestyles, those working and living in the country illegally, and basically anyone who has a worldview that says whatever you believe and however you want to live has to be tolerated. The popular thought in our culture is that if you disagree with someone, that makes you intolerant. The problem is that most people don't really understand what it means to tolerate something.*

To tolerate something—a belief or a point of view—means that you allow it to exist, even though you don't agree with it or like it. If I were truly intolerant, I would try to silence other points of view and eliminate them. But just because I disagree with someone doesn't mean I'm intolerant. What people who are pushing the tolerance agenda really want is to be helped and given special rights to live out their beliefs. It's really not about tolerance; rather, it's about truth. What are you doing to clear up the confusion?

"You yourselves know how unlawful it is for a man who is a Jew to associate with a foreigner or to visit him; and *yet* God has shown me that I should not call any man unholy or unclean."

ACTS 10:28 NASB

"Do not judge others, and you will not be judged."

MATTHEW 7:1 NLT

Finally, all of you, have unity of mind, sympathy, brotherly love, a tender heart, and a humble mind. Do not repay evil for evil or reviling for reviling, but on the contrary, bless, for to this you were called, that you may obtain a blessing. For "Whoever desires to love life and see good days, let him keep his tongue from evil and his lips from speaking deceit; let him turn away from evil and do good; let him seek peace and pursue it."

1 PETER 3:8–11 ESV

Jesus bent down and wrote with his finger in the dirt. They kept at him, badgering him. He straightened up and said, "The sinless one among you, go first: Throw the stone."

JOHN 8:6–7 MSG

He has been very kind and patient, waiting for you to change, but you think nothing of his kindness. Perhaps you do not understand that God is kind to you so you will change your hearts and lives.

ROMANS 2:4 NCV

TRUST

APP: *Every day we end up trusting a lot of different people and things. Every time I get on a plane to travel someplace, I'm having faith that the pilot knows how to fly the plane. Have you ever gone into a restaurant and performed tests on the food before you eat it? Not! Or how about testing the chair in your classroom at school before you sit down in it? Not! We trust something or someone because we have experienced their trustworthiness. But it only takes one bad experience to make you paranoid. I was in a bad car accident when a friend of mine was driving. That accident has turned me into a freaked-out passenger sometimes. Who or what do you trust? Why? Do you trust God? Some people say they trust God with their eternal destiny, but they have difficulty trusting Him with everyday things. Why is it hard to trust God with daily stuff? Probably the main reason is that we don't know Him very well. This causes us to have doubt that God is able to do what He promises and will always do what is best for us.*

Then Christ will make his home in your hearts as you trust in him.

EPHESIANS 3:17 NLT

Trust in the LORD with all your heart, and do not lean on your own understanding.

PROVERBS 3:5 ESV

Commit everything you do to the LORD. Trust him, and he will help you. He will make your innocence radiate like the dawn, and the justice of your cause will shine like the noonday sun.
PSALM 37:5–6 NLT

But those who trust in the LORD will find new strength. They will soar high on wings like eagles. They will run and not grow weary. They will walk and not faint.

ISAIAH 40:31 NLT

"Blessed is the man who trusts in the LORD and whose trust is the LORD."

JEREMIAH 17:7 NASB

Keep on doing what is right, and trust your lives to the God who created you, for he will never fail you.

1 PETER 4:19 NLT

TRUTH

APP: *There seems to be a lot of confusion today about what's fantasy and what's reality. Virtual Reality rides and games can make it possible for us to experience some pretty awesome things. Reality TV makes it possible to encounter some pretty strange people and situations. But maybe these kinds of shows are popular because people are searching for truth in their own lives. This search has been going on for generations.*

One of the disciples was confused as he tried to make sense out of the issues and mysteries of life. He finally questioned Jesus but didn't appear to be ready for His answer. Jesus told him that He is the truth. Philosophers say that truth is an idea, but Jesus challenged this way of thinking by stating that truth is a person.

Truth—the reality of an indisputable fact—is narrow by definition. Why is it so easy to apply ways of thinking to things like math and physics but hard to do in our relationship with God? The way that Jesus lived proves that He is completely reliable in all that He says and does. Knowing this should be an encouragement to us in our search for reality.

Study *and* be eager *and* do your utmost to present yourself to God approved (tested by trial), a workman who has no cause to be ashamed, correctly analyzing *and* accurately dividing [rightly handling and skillfully teaching] the Word of Truth.

2 TIMOTHY 2:15 AMPC

Finally, brothers, whatever is true, whatever is honorable, whatever is just, whatever is pure, whatever is lovely, whatever is commendable, if there is any excellence, if there is anything worthy of praise, think about these things.

PHILIPPIANS 4:8 ESV

But in every way we show we are servants of God: in accepting many hard things, in troubles, in difficulties, and in great problems. . . .by speaking the truth, and by God's power. We use our right living to defend ourselves against everything.

2 CORINTHIANS 6:4, 7 NCV

"And you will know the truth, and the truth will set you free."

JOHN 8:32 ESV

"God is spirit, and those who worship Him must worship in spirit and truth."

JOHN 4:24 NASB

The LORD detests lying lips, but he delights in those who tell the truth.

PROVERBS 12:22 NLT

UNCERTAINTY

APP: *We live in very uncertain times—massive earthquakes, tsunamis, school shootings, the war against terrorism, and our financial system in deep trouble. Add to these things unrealistic expectations from teachers, coaches, parents, and friends—it's no wonder life seems pretty freaky right now. It's like living in a constant state of doubt. With limited understanding of so many relationships, situations, and things around us, it's tough to have a lot of confidence about life when everything around us seems to be tentative. No wonder friends and family members are looking for a way to escape and survive the uncertainty of life in the twenty-first century. If we can't feel secure, maybe we can at least feel good. But this kind of attitude about life isn't something we should have if we have put our faith and trust in Jesus. Our confidence should be in Him and His Word. He is our rock and has proven that we can rely on Him—even in the middle of the crazy world that we live in. Our data about the times that we live in may be very limited, but God has all the facts.*

"This age continues until all these things take place. Sky and earth will wear out; my words won't wear out. But the exact day and hour? No one knows that, not even heaven's angels, not even the Son. Only the Father knows."

Matthew 24:35-36 MSG

Trust the Lord with all your heart, and
don't depend on your own understanding.
Remember the Lord in all you do,
and he will give you success.
Proverbs 3:5-6 NCV

Now faith is confidence in what we hope for and assurance about what we do not see.

Hebrews 11:1 NIV

Yet I am confident I will see the Lord's goodness while I am here in the land of the living.

Psalm 27:13 NLT

For I am confident of this very thing, that He who began a good work in you will perfect it until the day of Christ Jesus.

Philippians 1:6 NASB

For God is not *the author* of confusion but of peace.

1 Corinthians 14:33 NKJV

VAMPIRES

APP: *Vampires are a pop culture phenomenon. Real or fantasy, there are people who've bought into this way of life and developed a morbid taste for blood. They're not like Hollywood's Dracula or Edward. These people have been deceived into believing that they've been changed and now possess immortality and supernatural powers. They believe they have a capacity to absorb, channel, and manipulate "pranic energy" (life force). Vampire beliefs are really about power and searching for it from a source other than God. It's important to guard against the blurring of fantasy and reality that becomes hard to distinguish in real life.*

The word vampire is never mentioned in the Bible. But God does talk a lot about blood and power. Blood is sacred to God, and the devil is perverting its meaning and importance, deceiving some people into thinking that by drinking blood they can get power. Only the living God can give us the power we need.

Are vampires nibbling away at your time, energy, and passion? There's nothing wrong with fantasy unless you become so consumed with it that you're having trouble in the real world with real people. How about your relationship with Jesus? Has it taken a backseat to Bella, Edward, and Jacob? Think about the amazing unconditional love and ultimate sacrifice Jesus made for you.

"If any one of the house of Israel or of the strangers who sojourn among them eats any blood, I will set my face against that person who eats blood and will cut him off from among his people. For the life of the flesh is in the blood, and I have given it for you on the altar to make atonement for your souls, for it is the blood that makes atonement by the life. Therefore I have said to the people of Israel, No person among you shall eat blood, neither shall any stranger who sojourns among you eat blood. Any one also of the people of Israel, or of the strangers who sojourn among them, who takes in hunting any beast or bird that may be eaten shall pour out its blood and cover it with earth. For the life of every creature is its blood: its blood is its life. Therefore I have said to the people of Israel, You shall not eat the blood of any creature, for the life of every creature is its blood. Whoever eats it shall be cut off."

LEVITICUS 17:10–14 ESV

"Since they shed the blood of your holy people and your prophets, you have given them blood to drink. It is their just reward." REVELATION 16:6 NLT

You cannot drink the cup of the Lord and the cup of demons. You cannot partake of the table of the Lord and the table of demons.

1 CORINTHIANS 10:21 ESV

VENGEANCE

APP: *There's a lot of sorrow with this generation. People are especially hurt and angry over the way they've been treated by others. Broken lives are all around us. Sometimes it feels like we're walking through a battlefield on our campuses and in our neighborhoods. It's like there is carnage all over the place. Some want to take action to retaliate and avenge what's been done to them or someone they care about. People are looking for power to get vengeance on those who have hurt them. Our culture says we have the right to cause injury, harm, or humiliation on that person—that we should seek justice for the wrongs committed. This is a big theme in movies as we see "good guys" really being "bad guys" as they get their payback for the wrongs that have been committed. But the Bible teaches that we have to leave vengeance up to God. As we study God's Word, we also learn that vengeance is the opposite of forgiveness, which should be part of our character as we live for and like Jesus. Leaving vengeance in the hands of the Lord may be the hardest thing we ever do. But it's the right thing to do.*

Dear friends, never take revenge. Leave that to the righteous anger of God. For the Scriptures say, "I will take revenge; I will pay them back," says the LORD.

ROMANS 12:19 NLT

"Don't seek revenge or carry a grudge against any of your people. Love your neighbor as yourself. I am GOD."

LEVITICUS 19:18 MSG

Do not gloat when your enemy falls; when they stumble, do not let your heart rejoice.

PROVERBS 24:17 NIV

Do not say, "I will do to him as he has done to me; I will pay the man back for what he has done."

PROVERBS 24:29 ESV

He was beaten, he was tortured, but he didn't say a word. Like a lamb taken to be slaughtered and like a sheep being sheared, he took it all in silence. Justice miscarried, and he was led off—and did anyone really know what was happening?
ISAIAH 53:7 MSG

VIOLENCE

APP: *Violence can happen in lots of places and different situations. We see it so much in movies and TV shows that we've almost become desensitized to it. Violence can erupt across a country, on city streets, on a school campus, or in a home, causing amazing damage. Millions are victimized each year by rape, assault, and theft. The outcome can even lead to war and genocide where countless people are hurt and killed. It's scary to realize that we live in a culture where certain "acts" are no longer even considered violent by some people. What's the source? Where does this expression of physical or verbal force against self and others come from? The answer might surprise you. It's the human heart. It leans toward all kinds of sin, including violence, from the day we are born. There is a way to bring an end to the terrible violence in our world today. It starts with each person experiencing a spiritual heart transplant from God. He is the only One who knows what violence the human heart is capable of and who can transform it for good. What can you do—with God's help—to curb violence in your part of the world?*

But Jesus told him, "Put your sword away. Anyone who lives by fighting will die by fighting. Don't you know that I could ask my Father, and right away he would send me more than twelve armies of angels? But then, how could the words of the Scriptures come true, which say that this must happen?"

MATTHEW 26:52–54 CEV

The LORD examines both the righteous and the wicked. He hates those who love violence.

PSALM 11:5 NLT

"Do no wrong and do no violence to the stranger, the fatherless, or the widow, nor shed innocent blood in this place."
JEREMIAH 22:3 NKJV

Don't envy violent people or copy their ways.

PROVERBS 3:31 NLT

"Stop your violence and oppression and do what is just and right."

EZEKIEL 45:9 NLT

"The God of my strength, in whom I will trust; my shield and the horn of my salvation, my stronghold and my refuge; my Savior, You save me from violence."

2 SAMUEL 22:3 NKJV

VIOLENCE

APP: *Violence can happen in lots of places and different situations. We see it so much in movies and TV shows that we've almost become desensitized to it. Violence can erupt across a country, on city streets, on a school campus, or in a home, causing amazing damage. Millions are victimized each year by rape, assault, and theft. The outcome can even lead to war and genocide where countless people are hurt and killed. It's scary to realize that we live in a culture where certain "acts" are no longer even considered violent by some people. What's the source? Where does this expression of physical or verbal force against self and others come from? The answer might surprise you. It's the human heart. It leans toward all kinds of sin, including violence, from the day we are born. There is a way to bring an end to the terrible violence in our world today. It starts with each person experiencing a spiritual heart transplant from God. He is the only One who knows what violence the human heart is capable of and who can transform it for good. What can you do—with God's help—to curb violence in your part of the world?*

But Jesus told him, "Put your sword away. Anyone who lives by fighting will die by fighting. Don't you know that I could ask my Father, and right away he would send me more than twelve armies of angels? But then, how could the words of the Scriptures come true, which say that this must happen?"

MATTHEW 26:52–54 CEV

The LORD examines both the righteous and the wicked. He hates those who love violence.

PSALM 11:5 NLT

"Do no wrong and do no violence to the stranger, the fatherless, or the widow, nor shed innocent blood in this place."
JEREMIAH 22:3 NKJV

Don't envy violent people or copy their ways.
PROVERBS 3:31 NLT

"Stop your violence and oppression and do what is just and right."

EZEKIEL 45:9 NLT

"The God of my strength, in whom I will trust; my shield and the horn of my salvation, my stronghold and my refuge; my Savior, You save me from violence."
2 SAMUEL 22:3 NKJV

WAR

APP: *Since the end of World War II, there has not been a single twenty-four-hour period of time when there has not been violent conflict on this planet we call home. War is brutal and ugly, but it remains a significant part of human history and social change. It's broad and therefore is not linked to any one culture or society. In early human history, war was more like small-scale raiding. Today it has morphed into an organized violent conflict between two or more groups. And in all cases, at least one participant in the conflict perceives the need to dominate another. Usually the objective is to alter the mental, emotional, or material order between the groups at war. Usually the group experiencing the need to dominate is unable or unwilling to accept the possibility of a relationship of basic equality to exist with the other group. Power and control are what it's all about. War is different from genocide because of the give-and-take type of violent struggle and somewhat organized way that the groups are involved. God wants nations and people to live at peace with one another.*

"And you will hear of wars and rumors of wars. See that you are not alarmed, for this must take place, but the end is not yet."

MATTHEW 24:6 ESV

There is a time to love and a time to hate. There is a time for war and a time for peace.

ECCLESIASTES 3:8 NCV

I urge you, first of all, to pray for all people. Ask God to help them; intercede on their behalf, and give thanks for them. Pray this way for kings and all who are in authority so that we can live peaceful and quiet lives marked by godliness and dignity.

1 TIMOTHY 2:1–2 NLT

Be a good citizen. All governments are under God. Insofar as there is peace and order, it's God's order.

ROMANS 13:1 MSG

"Let the name of God be blessed forever and ever, for wisdom and power belong to Him. It is He who changes the times and the epochs; He removes kings and establishes kings; He gives wisdom to wise men and knowledge to men of understanding."

DANIEL 2:20–21 NASB

WICCA / WITCHCRAFT
(see also Sorcery)

APP: *Wicca is a complicated, contemporary religion that is often associated with occultism, neo-paganism, and witchcraft. Wicca, also known as witchcraft or the "craft of the wise," is a centuries-old religion. It emphasizes worship of the earth, all living creatures, and both the god and goddess. In Wicca, one also chooses the form of deity they work with, based on one's personal preferences, and what they want to work on. They have the freedom to custom design the kind of god they want to worship. It's a buffet-style, individually practiced religion. Since they make their own gods (deities), the gods are smaller and less powerful than they are, so Wicca is really about worshipping oneself because the self is in charge. At the heart of Wicca is a central rule called "The Rede," which says "Harm no one, do what you will." Basically, witches have the total freedom to do whatever seems right to them as long as they don't harm themselves or anyone else. There are no absolutes in Wicca. What should our response as Christians be to witchcraft, based on what the Bible teaches? Do you have a friend who is messing around with witchcraft? How does God want you to respond and help this person?*

"Do not defile yourselves by turning to mediums or to those who consult the spirits of the dead. I am the Lord your God."

Leviticus 19:31 NLT

When you enter the land the Lord your God is giving you, do not learn to imitate the detestable ways of the nations there. Let no one be found among you who sacrifices their son or daughter in the fire, who practices divination or sorcery, interprets omens, engages in witchcraft, or casts spells, or who is a medium or spiritist or who consults the dead. Anyone who does these things is detestable to the Lord; because of these same detestable practices the Lord your God will drive out those nations before you. You must be blameless before the Lord your God.

Deuteronomy 18:9–13 NIV

"You must not eat anything with the blood in it. You must not try to tell the future by signs or black magic."

Leviticus 19:26 NCV

"I will destroy your witchcraft and you will no longer cast spells."

Micah 5:12 NIV

WORRY

APP: *Most of us experience short-lived times of worry in our lives. It's a common emotion that causes us to be uneasy about something real or imagined. It's usually focused on things like being accepted, relationships, money, health, personal safety, or even environmental issues. Sometimes worry can have positive effects on us, causing us to avoid risky behavior or unhealthy friendships. But usually worry—especially if it's excessive—isn't good for us. For starters, it's a huge time waster. We can end up spending hours and hours worrying about something that may or may not ever happen. That time spent worrying is lost forever. We can never get it back again. Worrying also doesn't really accomplish anything. It can even make us physically sick. Worrying is the complete opposite of trusting God. It puts our eyes on the wrong place. We can try to use tricks or crazy gimmicks to stop us from worrying, but nothing can compare with the peace that comes from trusting God. He wants us to bring the things that make us worry and give them to Him to take care of.*

Do not be anxious about anything, but in everything by prayer and supplication with thanksgiving let your requests be made known to God.

PHILIPPIANS 4:6 ESV

"Seek first God's kingdom and what God wants. Then all your other needs will be met as well. So don't worry about tomorrow, because tomorrow will have its own worries. Each day has enough trouble of its own."
MATTHEW 6:33–34 NCV

And this same God who takes care of me will supply all your needs from his glorious riches, which have been given to us in Christ Jesus.

PHILIPPIANS 4:19 NLT

Be humble in the presence of God's mighty power, and he will honor you when the time comes. God cares for you, so turn all your worries over to him.
1 PETER 5:6–7 CEV

"Do not fear, for I am with you; do not anxiously look about you, for I am your God. I will strengthen you, surely I will help you, surely I will uphold you with My righteous right hand."

ISAIAH 41:10 NASB

YOUNG / YOUTH

APP: *The time between being a child and an adult can be strange. Changes with our bodies and emotions can make us feel as if we're riding on a gigantic roller coaster. It's easy to get frustrated and tired of hearing your grandparents say stuff like "Wait until you get older" or your aunt say, "Dear, when I was your age. . ." We have to be careful we don't waste the time in our lives when we are young, because we can make a difference if we really want to. At the core of every major movement in human history have been young people. Most of the time good things have happened. But sometimes movements like Hitler's Nazi Youth led to a nightmare. Keep in mind that just because you're young doesn't mean you're immature. And just because you're an adult doesn't mean you're automatically mature. Our world needs change, but more has to happen than building a movement around information technology or political and social action. All of this can be good, but it won't be enough without a spiritual foundation for the movement. Dream big dreams of how God can use you, surrender them to Him, work on growing spiritually, and see what happens. God has used youth to change history, and there's still much to be done.*

Let no one despise you for your youth, but set the believers an example in speech, in conduct, in love, in faith, in purity.

1 Timothy 4:12 esv

Don't let the excitement of youth cause you to forget your Creator. Honor him in your youth before you grow old and say, "Life is not pleasant anymore."

Ecclesiastes 12:1 nlt

My child, do not forget my teaching, but keep my commands in mind. Then you will live a long time, and your life will be successful. Don't ever forget kindness and truth. Wear them like a necklace. Write them on your heart as if on a tablet. Then you will be respected and will please both God and people. Trust the Lord with all your heart, and don't depend on your own understanding. Remember the Lord in all you do, and he will give you success. Don't depend on your own wisdom. Respect the Lord and refuse to do wrong.

Proverbs 3:1–7 ncv

Some people brought their little children to Jesus so he could touch them, but his followers told them to stop. When Jesus saw this, he was upset and said to them, "Let the little children come to me. Don't stop them, because the kingdom of God belongs to people who are like these children. I tell you the truth, you must accept the kingdom of God as if you were a little child, or you will never enter it." Then Jesus took the children in his arms, put his hands on them, and blessed them.

Mark 10:13–16 ncv

The Power to Change Your Life

Understanding the topics and verses in this book are important to help us make sense of what we experience in life and get the answers we need. The verses themselves are different from the words we can find on the pages of other books. They contain supernatural power because they are God's words. They're awesome because they have the energy to radically transform the way we live. But before this can happen, we have to change the way we think and the way we live. It's not enough just to know about God; we need to have a personal relationship with Him. God must accomplish something in us before He does anything for us and through us. He must cure the disease that we are all born with. It's much worse than AIDS or cancer, and it's terminal.

It's a spiritual disease called sin that we inherited from the first man and woman—Adam and Eve (Genesis 3). This disease was passed on from generation to generation until it reached us. The Bible tells us in Romans 3:23 that everyone has sinned and fallen short of God's superb, holy standard. Sin is wrong thoughts, words, and actions according to God's standards. At its very core, sin is living in rebellion against God and attempting to live our life without Him. For some people this rebellion is fleshed out in an out-of-control lifestyle, while for others it's just quietly ignoring God and His existence. Either way, the consequences of sin are disastrous and deadly (Romans 6:23).

Sin is not a word we'd use in a text message or talking with a friend. But it's something that we see the effects of every day in our families, on our campuses, and in the world that we live in. Sin hurts us, others in our life, and even God. It separates us from Him and keeps us from experiencing a satisfying life. In order for God to heal us from this illness, He had to do something extreme and unimaginable—sacrifice His only Son, Jesus, on a cross. This was the only way possible for us to be forgiven and have our relationship with Him restored. It was an amazing expression of His unconditional love for us. "But God showed his great love for us by sending Christ to die for us while we were still sinners" (Romans 5:8 NLT). We can be forgiven and become a new person because Jesus died for our sin and rose from the grave.

Sin is ugly—it stinks, and it keeps us from having a relationship with our Father in heaven. No matter how many verses we read in the Bible, how many good things we might accomplish, or how much we go to church, it's not enough to satisfy a holy God for our rebellion against Him. Check out Isaiah 59:2: "It's your sins that have cut you off from God. Because of your sins, he has turned away and will not listen anymore" (NLT).

Jesus gave us the answer when He said that we need to repent of our sins and turn to God (Luke 13:3). When the Bible was written, if a person saw someone going in the wrong direction, he would say to that person, "Repent," which meant "turn around, turn back because you're going the wrong way." Today when Jesus says, "Repent," He's instructing us to turn away from our self-centeredness and self-control to allow Him to be in charge and give direction.

When we repent, it means that we regret what we have done in the past and feel sorry for rebelling against God and trying to live without Him. There will be such a sense of brokenness that we will hate our sin. Then we will recognize that we desperately need Jesus and will surrender our lives to Him. Giving up control of our lives to Jesus is a hard thing to do, but it's a sign that we really do want to change the way we're living and need His help to accomplish it. We are willing to live our lives for and like Him.

If we make this decision, the payback is amazing! God totally and completely forgives us for our sin—all of it. He makes us new people and adopts us into His forever family. We receive God's gift of eternal life with Him, hope, courage, and a purpose for living. From the moment we give up control to Jesus, we can be confident of His direction and answers for our lives. It takes faith and trust.

But be aware that it will cost you. The price to repent and surrender is heavy. It could involve everything, from your dreams for the future to relationships, to your very life. But no matter what happens, you can be assured that God has an awesome plan and a purpose in it all (Jeremiah 29:11; 1 Corinthians 2:9).

Maybe you've read parts of the Bible before or even read it cover to cover. The power of God's Word will have no lasting effect on you until you decide to accept what Jesus did on the cross for you, turn from your sin, and surrender your life to Him.

If you've become aware of your sin and want to repent and surrender, here's how you might want to pray:

Lord Jesus, I recognize that I was born in sin and need Your forgiveness. I want to turn away from my sin and surrender my life to You. I believe You died for my sin and came back to life after three days.

Please come into my life, take control, and help me
to become the person You created me to be.
Thank You for Your love. I want to live my life
for and like You. In Jesus' name. Amen.

If you made the decision to surrender your life to Jesus and live your life for and like Him, let me know. You can e-mail me through our Web site, realanswers. com, or text me the words "go live" to 411247.

I'd like to help you get started on your spiritual journey with Jesus by sending you some materials that will help you grow in your love for God and for people (Matthew 22:37–39).

Contact the Author

Steve Russo
PO Box 1549
Ontario, California 91762

Phone: 909.466.7060
Text: GoLive to 411247
Email: steve@steverusso.com

realanswers.com
steverusso.com
utalkradio.com

Facebook@steverussodrummer
Instagram: @steverussoofficial
Twitter: @steverusso1
Snapchat: @Cooldrumguy4
YouTube: @steverussodrummer

About the Author

Steve Russo is a prolific author, professional drummer, radio/TV host, and speaker. He's been featured on ABC, CBS, and NBC news broadcasts. Steve loves Italian food, Moose Tracks ice cream, and the Los Angeles Lakers. His favorite place to visit is Italy, but he also likes to hang out at the beach in northern California. Steve is a graduate of Biola University and the Arrow Leadership Program. Don't tell anyone—he was a tap dancer in elementary school.

Bible Permissions

Notes

_____

_____

_____

_____

_____

_____

_____

_____

_____

_____

_____

_____

_____

Notes

Notes

_____

_____

_____

_____

_____

_____

_____

_____

_____

_____

_____

_____

_____

Notes

Notes